EDMUND FREDERIK DU CANE

AF859842

# THE PUNISHMENT

AND

# PREVENTION OF CRIME

Elibron Classics
www.elibron.com

Elibron Classics series.



ISBN 0-543-96753-0 (paperback)
ISBN 0-543-96752-2 (hardcover)

This Elibron Classics Replica Edition is an unabridged facsimile of the edition published in 1885 by Macmillan and Co., London.

# The Punishment
## and
# Prevention of Crime

THE ENGLISH CITIZEN:

*HIS RIGHTS AND RESPONSIBILITIES.*

# THE PUNISHMENT

AND

# PREVENTION OF CRIME


BY

COL. SIR EDMUND F. DU CANE,

K.C.B., R.E.

CHAIRMAN OF COMMISSIONERS OF PRISONS,

CHAIRMAN OF DIRECTORS OF PRISONS, INSPECTOR-GENERAL OF MILITARY PRISONS,

SURVEYOR-GENERAL OF PRISONS



London

MACMILLAN AND CO.

1885

*Printed by* R. & R. Clark, *Edinburgh.*

# CONTENTS.

## CHAPTER I.



## CHAPTER II.



## CHAPTER III.



## CHAPTER IV.



## CHAPTER V.

## CHAPTER VI.



## CHAPTER VII.



## CHAPTER VIII.

# THE PUNISHMENT

AND

# PREVENTION OF CRIME

# THE PUNISHMENT

AND

# PREVENTION OF CRIME.

## CHAPTER I.

### CRIMINALS AND PUNISHMENTS.

CRIME may very well be compared with physical disease, and the mode of proceeding for repression of the one is in principle the same as for the other. The most effective mode is to remove its causes, which often have their origin in our social condition, and more often in the absence or weakening of those moral restraints by means of which society is kept together. But when this mode fails, or when we omit, from want of knowledge or other cause, to apply it, we are obliged, for the protection of the community, to resort to such methods of *curing* it as may prove most effectual. According to the principles which have long been accepted in England, these methods must be founded on a combination of penal and reformatory elements applied in their proper circumstances, and in their due proportions.

The object of the penal element is more to deter

others than for the effect on the individual subjected to the punishment. In accordance with the observation addressed by a Heath judge to a criminal on whom he was passing sentence—"You are sentenced to be hanged, not because you stole the horse, but in order to prevent others from stealing horses." On this subject the *Report of the Directors of Convict Prisons*, 1873, contains the following observations:—"When everything has been done to deter from crime or reform the criminal there will still remain a certain class whom it is hopeless to influence, and who must be dealt with in course of law, not for much result on themselves, but to carry out the principle of justice, and mainly to deter others. Such characters may probably be set down as in a certain sense mentally deficient. The following extracts from a paper by Dr. Nicholson in the *Journal of Mental Science* points out this peculiarity of the criminal mind, and supports the idea, which has been elsewhere broached, that the fact of certain prisoners being repeatedly reconvicted is no proof that the system of a prison is defective; the truth being that if by punishing those who have an incurable tendency to crime we can deter fresh recruits from joining the ranks of the criminal class, the object of punishment is effected; and obviously if we could possibly arrive at the result that all convictions were re-convictions, and none of them first sentences, we should be in a fair way to putting an end to crime altogether.

"And this quality of reflection is certainly feebly represented in criminals generally. Many of them do not, and some possibly cannot, comprehend their own position or realise their true self-interest as social and responsible beings; and their actions are but too frequently prompted by what appears to them the expediency of the moment. Speaking proverbially, they form a class of fools whom even experience fails to teach. The lessons of the past profit them not as guides for the future. Apart from the question of their natural proneness to evil, the frequent misdemeanours of criminals, whether in prison or out of it, in spite of such punishment as ought to prove deterrent, is either an evidence of a strange indifference to pain or else it shows that the impression left by the punishment, if it has not faded altogether, is at least so weakened as to be useless even if recalled when the individual is again about to commit himself; *i.e.* the memory has no record of the pain, or the feeble residue which it preserves of it goes for nothing in the face of the emotion or other cause of misconduct.

"Professor Bain, working out the balance of actual and ideal motives in reference to the repeated commission of crime, says:—'We must suppose, what is probably true of the criminal class generally, a low retentiveness for good and evil the analytic expression of imprudence, perhaps the most radically incurable of all natural defects.' This formula, 'a low retentiveness for good and evil,' is well adapted to form a groundwork for the explanation of many of the vicious displays of imprisoned criminals. It implies scant powers of reflection, and indicates a state of moral weakness and possibly of moral depravity; and upon such a basis a healthy or strong exercise of the will can hardly be looked for. Hence it follows that in some cases even an ordinary emotion, in the absence of the moderating influence which a deliberative volition should exert, leads to the commission of acts as unreasonable and as destructive as those committed at the instigation of a violent emotional impulse, whose course an ordinary will is found to be incapable of resisting or controlling."

An examination of the criminal population as a whole has led some skilled observers to express the opinion that in mental and bodily constitution male prisoners are below the average of the population of which they form a part; and the same may be said of female prisoners though in a less marked degree. It must, however, be admitted that while the general criminal population may be thus described, there are always to be found among criminals, in prison or out, a number of persons of great skill and cleverness, qualities which, since they are not restrained by any moral considerations, tempt them perhaps to measure themselves against the law, but which fortunately do not always and completely protect them; for their own moral defects, such as indolence, dissipation, treachery, etc., help to defeat their combinations and restore the balance in favour of the community. There is also good foundation for the observation that the able and intelligent criminal seeks the aid of the weaker-minded men and women in his enterprises, and contrives sometimes that they shall suffer in his place. The weak-minded, insane, and epileptic criminals are specially addicted to certain crimes, such as arson, and to crimes indicating a preponderance of the animal nature, often marked by violence. And both these two classes of incurable criminals, the one who deliberately adopts a course of crime in reliance on his own power of evading detection, and the other who is a criminal because he is weak-minded or imbecile, must be dealt with on different principles from those others who may by appropriate treatment be deterred or reformed.

The connection between age and the tendency to crime is worthy of attention. In a census of the convict prison population in 1873, it was shown that, whereas the ages of the general population above fifteen years are in the following proportions :—

| | Proportion per cent. | | | | | |
|---|---|---|---|---|---|---|
| | 15 to 24 years inclusive. | 25 to 34 years. | 35 to 44 years. | 45 to 54 years. | 55 to 64 years. | 65 years and upwards. |
| Males . | 29·3 | 22·9 | 17·7 | 13·9 | 9·2 | 7·0 |
| Females | 28·4 | 23·2 | 17·7 | 13·7 | 9·3 | 7·7 |

the ages of the population of the convict prisons are as follows :—

| | | | | | | |
|---|---|---|---|---|---|---|
| Males . | 27·2 | 39·7 | 19·2 | 8·5 | 3·8 | 1·6 |
| Females | 15·4 | 41·7 | 23·8 | 12·7 | 5·3 | 1·0 |

It appears, therefore, that that part of the population which is between twenty-five and thirty-four supplies far more than its proper proportion to the convict prisons. This may therefore be called the "criminal age." It appears also that the criminal age begins and ends later in females than in males.

These observations are confirmed by an analysis made in the present year, and it appears from a similar analysis of the population of the Local Prisons that in them persons between twenty and thirty are in an unduly large proportion.

The fact of the large decrease of crime continuously after the age of thirty-four is well worthy of note; whether it arises from the moral feelings being in some individuals developed later than ordinarily, or in a desire after a certain age for a quieter life than the risk and excitement of crime can offer; but it would seem to warrant the inference that a vast amount of crime would be put an end to if those persons whose career evidences in them marked criminal tendencies could either be locked up or kept under supervision until they had passed, say the age of forty, supplying thus in the interest of the public that self-control in which they are obviously deficient, for there can be little doubt that most of the undetected crime—which much exceeds that which is followed by punishment—is committed by persons of this class. Many of them might thenceforward become respectable members of society.

It is also worthy of observation that the proportion of male convicts convicted of serious crime is much larger than females, in fact 9 to 1; the proportion of males to females convicted of minor crimes is only 4 to 1.

The explanation of this probably is that the occupation of females is not generally such as to lead them to commit those offences against morals which bring them under the operation of the criminal law, and especially does not expose them in an equal degree to the danger of committing the more serious offences.

The conditions of the problem will, on the whole, be found to justify the conclusion that reformatory influences should predominate in dealing with the younger criminals, those whose minds and character are still unformed and undeveloped; that in the older and more hardened the penal element should have the *first* place—both on account of its effect on themselves and its influence in deterring others; and that for incorrigibles the only mode of protecting society against them is that they should be entirely removed from temptation which they cannot withstand, and be made use of as examples to others.

As to the amount of punishment which should be inflicted it is probable that nothing can be prescribed further than that it should be the least amount which will effect the above objects; and from this point of view the stereotyped custom of assigning the periods of 5, 7, 10, 14, and 21 years' penal servitude (a custom no doubt derived from the days of actual transportation), to the exclusion of the intermediate periods of years, is difficult to justify, and may even defeat the great object; for there is much evidence to prove that, after six or seven years, the deterrent effect diminishes on the prisoner who endures it, and is therefore likely to be less on those who hear his account after his discharge than if he had come out before getting used to his position. The use of certain stereotyped periods for sentences of imprisonment might perhaps also be reconsidered, for intermediate periods now very seldom made use of might no doubt often be sufficient for their purpose.

The punishments which now can be legally enforced are Death, Penal Servitude, Transportation, and Imprisonment with or without Hard Labour; Confinement in a Reformatory, Police Supervision, Whipping, Fine, Putting under Recognisances. To these should be added, as a preventive and not as a punishment for crime, Confinement in an Industrial School. Death being now inflicted on rare occasions and corporal punishment quite exceptionally, a description of our penal and preventive system is for the most part a description of the system adopted in the various institutions in which persons are confined for the purpose of checking crime.

It would be impossible to understand our present penal and preventive system, or to appreciate the reasons for many of its characteristics, without some knowledge of what has gone before, and of the experience on which it is founded.

Those who have been much engaged in practically conducting affairs of any magnitude will know how frequently it happens that every course which can be adopted has its attendant disadvantages, and that a judicious decision as to which course shall be followed is only to be arrived at by balancing the advantages and disadvantages of each. Nothing is more common than to find afterwards that persons whose attention has been attracted only to some disadvantage in the system finally decided on, discuss it without being aware that any alternative would introduce still greater evils. This consideration makes it the more desirable to record the steps by which the existing practice and system have grown up, to bring their results to the test of unimpeachable facts, and to show the various evils to which penal establishments are liable, and the errors which we must carefully endeavour to avoid in the further progress we should hope for and endeavour to effect.

## CHAPTER II.

### PUNISHMENTS IN THE MIDDLE AGES—CAPITAL EXECUTIONS.

THE punishments chiefly made use of by our forefathers were of the kind that are described as "short and sharp," though sometimes very durable in their effect on the person subjected to them. The Criminal Law, which no doubt the Romans introduced into and left in their islands, was remarkable in comparison with that which succeeded it for the mercy which tempered its justice—if the use of torture, and the punishments inflicted on slaves, and the punishments for witchcraft and parricide, are left out of consideration. They seem to have arrived at a level of humanity and good order which was not again touched in England till long after the present century had begun. Even in gaol the accused were not to be subject to any duress, nor were women to be imprisoned in the same room with men. The case of any prisoner was to be heard within a month; and even if a postponement was then asked for, it was in no case to extend beyond a year. By the laws of the twelve tables it appears that substantially Roman punishments consisted of death, fines or money compensation, flogging, and outlawry. A capital offence did not necessarily mean one which was punishable by death, but by loss of civil condition—degradation from freedom to slavery, or deprivation of the full privileges of citizenship, compulsory service in mines, and the working of the hand-mill and transportation were not uncommon.

Under Constantine most humane and enlightened principles prevailed. The judges were well looked after. Slaves might be chastised with a slender rod, but not with a cudgel. Convicts condemned to the games or to mines, which involved loss of freedom, might not be branded on the forehead, but on other parts of the body. Punishment by inflicting a mortal wound with a sharp weapon or by poison, torture, starving, hanging, mutilation, throwing from a height, were forbidden, "for these," said the Emperor, "are the cruelties of the ruthless barbarian."

With the invasion of the barbarians and the disappearance of Roman order and civilisation an entire change came over the spirit of the Government. Besides death, fines, and flogging, mutilation was a common punishment; men were branded on the forehead; their hands, feet, and tongues were cut off; and after the Danish invasion still more horrible mutilations were practised, though Canute enjoined them in order that "Christian men might not for too little be put to death, but rather to some gentle punishment." For the greater offences eyes were plucked out; the nose, ears, and upper lip were cut off; the scalp was torn off; a female slave guilty of theft was burned alive; and men were even flayed alive. William the Conqueror made provisions of much the same sort, also with the object of restricting the practice of hanging, though afterwards the ideas of humanity seem to have changed, and it was considered more merciful to hang a culprit than to cut off an important member. For many or most crimes, however, fines were inflicted in Saxon times on a first conviction, but death for a second; and for certain crimes death followed a first conviction, the mode of death decreed in Ethelred's laws being, "Let him be smitten till his neck brake."

Under the influence of the Roman Church clerics were exempted from punishment by lay courts, and so from capital punishment. Moreover, the rich could commute their punishments for a fine; and the persons and property of the rich were protected by heavier punishments on those who attacked them than the persons or property of the poor. The slaves incurred the punishment of death or mutilation for the most trifling offences.

In Sir James Stephen's *History of the Criminal Law*, from which I have gathered much valuable information, a clear account is given of the punishments formerly and now in force. Death was at common law the punishment for all felonies except petty larceny and mayhem. For misdemeanours fines, whipping, and imprisonment were the punishment. The claim of the Church to judge all clerics, known under the name of "benefit of clergy," led to the exemption of a large class of persons from the operation of the law imposing capital punishment on felons; for although at first applicable only to clerics it was afterwards extended to all who could read except women and a few others, and finally—1705—to all persons. But meanwhile the exemption itself had been taken away in the case of many crimes. This had been done to a considerable extent under the Tudors, and much more during the eighteenth century; but in the latter period capital convictions were generally followed by pardon conditional on transportation. In the reign of George IV. benefit of clergy was abolished entirely, and capital punishment also for many crimes which were excluded from benefit of clergy. But even when benefit of clergy was fully in force it could only be claimed for one offence, unless the criminal was actually in orders; and the first offence could easily be established by the brand M for murder, T for theft.

In mediæval times whipping, branding, mutilation, and dismemberment, and disgraceful public exposure, were the common physical punishments short of death. Those who refused to plead were, until 1772, pressed, *i.e.* heavy weights were placed on their prostrate bodies till they gave in or died; or in the time of Queen Anne their thumbs might be tied together till they entered their plea. From 1772 such persons were by law treated as guilty; but in 1827 the law provided that they should be treated as having pleaded "not guilty," and tried accordingly.

Branding was inflicted on convicts who claimed benefit of clergy when convicted of capital crimes, for which the sentence was hanging, and consisted in scaring the offender with hot iron on the brawn of the thumb, marking a murderer with M, and others T. In the reign of William and Mary the branding was directed to be on the most visible part of the left cheek, near the nose. Vagabonds were branded with a

V; idlers with S for slave. A church brawler lost his ears, and was branded F for fighter or fray-maker; sometimes a hole an inch in diameter was made in the gristle of the right ear.

Mutilations were sometimes inflicted with great cruelty. When an offender had his ears nailed to the pillory it was sometimes done so that by the motion of his body he was forced gradually to tear them off.

William Prynne lost his ears by sentence of the Star Chamber for seditious publications. The Earl of Dorset in pronouncing sentence expressed his personal opinion that he should be loth he should escape with his ears, "Therefore I would have him branded in the forehead, slit in the nose, and his ears cropt too." Three years later he lost the remainder of his ears, and was branded S L—seditious libeller—on both cheeks.

Mutilation was, however, almost abandoned by the end of the sixteenth century, except that of cropping the ears; but late in the reign of Henry VIII. an Act was passed declaring that for striking so as to shed blood within the King's Court the penalty should be the loss of the right hand, as it had been for many crimes before the Conquest. The ceremony for carrying out this punishment was most carefully devised and elaborate, invoking the attendance and assistance of the sergeant of the woodyard to furnish the block and cords; the master cook to perform the operation; the sergeant of the larder, the sergeant of the poultry, and the yeoman of the scullery; the sergeant farrier, the chief surgeon, the groom of the salcey, the sergeant of the eury, and the yeoman of the chantry; the sergeant of the pantry and the sergeant of the cellar—all of whom performed certain services of comfort or cure to the unfortunate sufferer.

It was no doubt the remembrance of the legal infliction of the punishment of slitting the nose which suggested to some of the officers of Charles II.'s guard to waylay and punish Sir John Coventry in this way for some joke about the king's partiality for actresses, and this crime thenceforth, by an Act called the Coventry Act, was made felony, without benefit of clergy.

The pillory was in use much later on. Williams, the publisher, who reprinted Wilkes' *North Briton*, No. 45, stood in the pillory in 1765 for an hour. Lord Cochrane was sentenced to the same degradation in 1814, but the sentence was not carried out. It ceased to be a punishment, except for forgery, in 1815, and was applied in the case of Dr. Bossy in 1830; but in 1837 it was altogether abolished.

The stocks were a comparatively mild form of public disgrace. They are traced back to a statute of Edward III., in which they were declared to be a punishment for unruly labourers. Soon after every village had its stocks near the church, and brawlers, drunkards, vagrants, "hedge tearers," and other disorderly persons, were exposed in them, and it is said that in his hot youth Cardinal Wolsey occupied the distinguished position they offered. They were in use till 1860 at least, when one John Gamble of Stanningly, suffered this punishment for six hours for Sunday gambling.

For women scolds the branks or gag and the ducking-stool or tumbril were authorised punishments; and the ducking-stool was used at Leominster in 1809.

Fines, imprisonment, and whipping, are the punishments for misdemeanour by common law, though many misdemeanours are punishable by transportation and imprisonment with hard labour. The punishment of whipping was commonly awarded to men guilty of petty thefts. Women were whipped besides being put in the pillory. Usually women were flogged in private, but not always, even up till the end of the eighteenth century; the men in public, sometimes in the gate or the market-place of the town, or for 100 or 200 yards through the streets.

Whipping has never been abolished by statute, but practically is applied only in cases in which it is specially authorised by statute.

Justices in petty sessions may order a boy under fourteen to have twelve strokes with a birch rod for simple larceny or attempting to upset railway trains, and for certain offences under the Summary Jurisdiction Act, 1879.

Courts of assizes or quarter sessions may order a boy under sixteen to be whipped for certain indictable offences; the number of strokes and the weapon are not prescribed in the Act, but must be specified in the sentence. In 1863 an Act was passed under which a judge of assize might order boys over sixteen and men to be flogged for robbery with violence, or by two or more, or for attempting to choke (garroting). For any of these offences one, two, or three floggings may be ordered, as an addition to any other punishment, with an instrument not prescribed in the Act but to be specified in the sentence, the number of strokes not to exceed fifty. A boy under sixteen may be subjected to whipping for the same offences, the instrument to be a birch rod and the number of strokes not above twenty-five.

The punishment of death has been inflicted in various manners in different countries and in different periods, sometimes with great brutality and torture. In England the death penalty was carried out by hanging, burning, or the axe; only during a few years of Henry VIII.'s reign was boiling to death made lawful for poisoning. Burning was the punishment for heresy and for petty treason, viz., such crimes as the murder of a master by his servants, etc. It was thus inflicted on a woman for coining in 1788, and not till 1790 was the ordinary punishment of hanging substituted for it, though latterly the burning was mercifully preceded by hanging.

It is perhaps difficult for any person brought up among our modern ideas to realise the free use made of the penalty of hanging in the time of our forefathers down even till a very recent date. It is difficult to get at any statistical facts as to the number of persons so executed in remote times in any period; but Coke (in the time of Elizabeth) remarks on the large number of persons hanged, and seeing how the effect of punishment was weakened by its uncertainty, he observed that many offended on hope of pardon.

Sir James Stephen, in his work on the *History of Criminal Law*, quotes the Records of Assizes and Quarter Sessions at Exeter in 1598, and shows that in the calendar of that year there appear to have been 74 sentenced to be hanged in the year out of 387 tried. He says, "If we allow for each of the forty counties an average of only 20, this would give 800 persons hanged in the year in England." The population of England was then under

5,000,000. As giving a view of the mode of disposing of prisoners, the Record of Lent Assizes may be quoted. "At this there were 134 for trial—17 sentenced to be hanged, 20 flogged, 16 pardoned, 11 claimed benefit of clergy, and were branded and discharged."

In 1750 alarm created by the increase of crime rose to a panic; in the year following no less than 63 were hanged in London alone—the small London of those days. But Parliament could devise no better means of checking crime than by increasing the number of capital felonies. "If a country gentleman," said Burke, "can obtain no other favour from Government, he is sure to be accommodated with a new felony without benefit of clergy." In September 1783, 58 were sentenced to death at the Old Bailey, in December following 24. In Lent 1785 there were at Kingston 21 capital sentences and 9 executions; and at Gloucester 16 such sentences and 9 carried out; there were 7 executions at Warwick, 6 each at Winchester and Salisbury, and 5 at Shrewsbury. The total in England alone were 242, of whom 103 suffered.

The celebrated Bow Street runner, Townsend, in evidence given in 1816 before a Parliamentary committee, said that between 1781-87 he had seen as many as 12, 16, or 20 hanged at one execution. Twice he saw 40 hanged at one time. "Plunder had got to such an alarming pitch that a letter was circulated among the judges and recorders then sitting, that His Majesty would dispense with the recorders' reports, and that the most criminal should be at once picked out and ordered for execution."

Parliament, however, did not lose faith in their

remedy, and accordingly by 1797 the number of capital offences without benefit of clergy was 160, and it rose to 222, when the efforts of Sir S. Romilly for reform in this matter succeeded only so far as to have pocket-picking, which was capital if above one shilling, taken out of the list of capital offences. In 1811 he failed in his Bill for withdrawing the offence of stealing from bleaching-grounds from the list of crimes then punishable by hanging; and in 1812 the same ill success met his Bill relating to soldiers and sailors found begging: so also in 1813, 1816, 1818, he failed in his most moderate desire to abolish capital punishment for stealing to the value of 4s. from shops. In 1833 a child of nine was sentenced to be hanged for poking a stick through a patched-up pane of glass and stealing twopence-worth of paint, but he was not executed.

In 1829, however, thanks to the discussion of the question, the practice had been so far modified that only 24 were hanged in London for crimes other than murder.

Between 1832 and 1835 a sweeping and general change was at length made by immensely reducing the list of capital felonies, and further reductions were made in 1837 and 1841.

From 1832 to 1844 none were hanged for any other crime than murder. In 1861 the law was made to correspond with this practice by abolishing that punishment for seven other crimes which till then could legally be so punished, so that now murder and treason, piracy with violence, and setting fire to dockyards and arsenals, are the only crimes for which death can be pronounced.

Numerous, however, as were the capital executions in the times referred to, culprits being strung up in batches at Tyburn, it would be far from correct to suppose that a sentence of death was mostly followed by execution. In 1805 only 68 persons were hanged out of 350 sentenced to death; and though in 1831 no less than 1601 persons received that sentence it was only carried out in 52 cases, and of these 52 murder was the crime of 12 of the offenders.

The contrast between the punishment awarded and that which was actually endured if the capital sentence was commuted was almost ludicrous, and justifies Coke's opinion that criminals reckoned on the commutation, so that the penalty and sentences lost their terrors. For instance, of 17 persons capitally convicted at Newgate in 1835-36, 2 suffered, 2 had three months' imprisonment, and the rest various terms.

Sir James Stephen says that when all restrictions on benefit of clergy had been removed by the beginning of the eighteenth century the punishment for all common offences became slight. If a man was not hung he was discharged, or at most imprisoned for a year without hard labour.

It has been stated above that in 1833 the number of executions in England and Wales was 52; in 1831 it was 68; in 1836 it had fallen to 17, and from then to the end of 1883 there have been in the forty-seven years 557 persons executed, or an average of 12 a year nearly; the smallest number in any of these years was 4, in 1871; and the largest was 22 in each of the years 1863, 1876, and 1877. During these years the population of England and Wales has risen from 15,103,778 to

26,770,744. The course of the changes by which during this period the law has been brought more nearly to accord with the sentiments which governed the practice is very striking. In 1836, 1837, and 1838, there were 954 sentences to death but only 31 executions. Thence till 1862 there were 1395 sentences and 261 executions; thence till 1883 there were 524 sentences and 207 executions. While the population, therefore, has nearly doubled, the average number of executions has remained about the same, but the number of sentences has enormously decreased.

The carrying out of a sentence of execution is the duty of the sheriff, a privilege which has been reserved to them by successive Acts of Parliament, although the charge of the King's Prisons, which formerly was one of his duties, has been gradually withdrawn from him and vested in other authorities.

A culprit in England who was sentenced to be hanged used formerly to be taken on a cart to the place of execution, where a gallows had been erected, and the execution was effected by drawing away from under him the cart in which he was standing, after the rope had been fastened round his neck. Very frequently the place in which a murder was committed was selected as the scene of punishment; but in London for many years, and till the end of the eighteenth century, Tyburn was the place in which hanging was performed, except in the cases of pirates, who suffered at Execution Dock. The murderers were, by 25 Geo. II. cap. 27, only allowed one whole intervening day between sentence and execution, except when the sentences were passed on Friday, when the execution was to be on

Monday. During the interval they were fed on bread and water. So far as concerns Newgate, other criminals sentenced to be hanged were kept a long time in suspense as to their fate, as it had to be discussed and settled by the King in Council, so that the decision was seldom given in less than six weeks, and sometimes not for months. Once during the illness of George III. no less than 100 persons were in Newgate waiting the decision on their capital sentences.

In February 1817 Mr. Bennett found in Newgate 5 who had been sentenced in July previous, 4 in September, and 24 in October. During this period the prisoner led a dissolute, brutal life; the chances of his escaping the penalty were considerable, and surrounded as he was, in consequence of the state of prison construction and administration, by associates who gave themselves up to a life which violated all order and decency, and abandoned themselves to all the low pleasures which they could procure in gaol, he treated the sentence of death with habitual and inexpressible levity, threw in his lot with them, and sought their applause for his spirit and indifference to his fate. The chaplain, if he took any trouble about him, found that in such surroundings his efforts could be of no avail. He reserved his force for the condemned sermon, at which the prisoners whose sentences were not commuted attended, sitting round a coffin,—if they could not get off on some pretext an ordeal which they dreaded,—and when the chaplain held forth for their edification and that of the other prisoners who attended, and of the spectators who came to enjoy the cruel pleasure. This latter scandal was in 1825 put an end to at Newgate, but an exception was made for the last time in 1840 for the benefit of some sensation-loving persons, who desired to see the wretched Courvoisier on that occasion, a crowd of whom were admitted by ticket, including a few ladies. Some of the more callous or defiant prisoners gave a farewell dinner-party before they were hanged, dressed themselves with great care for the ceremony, were particular in such items as having "a white cockade" if in London, took their last drink at St. Giles', and took care to comport themselves on the long journey from Newgate to Tyburn and at the gallows so that spectators might say they "died game." The spectators came sometimes in great crowds, ribald, reckless, and brutal; sometimes sympathising with and cheering, sometimes execrating, deriding, or throwing missiles at the criminal, but little affected for any good purpose, for picking pockets went on under the gallows. The ordinary attended on the journey (sometimes an amateur would come and dispute with him the right to minister to the culprit), and when all was over made a profit by selling the account of the execution.

The scandalous scenes created by the procession, and the delay caused by the dense crowd lining the way and accompanying the cart (Lord Ferrars took a terrible three hours on account of the crowd all along the journey), led to the execution being ordered to take place in the great area before Newgate. This change was not without its opponents. Dr. Johnson observed, "Tyburn itself is not safe from the fury of innovation. Executions are intended to draw spectators; if they do not they do not answer their purpose. The old method was most satisfactory to all parties; the public was gratified by a procession, the criminal was supported by it. Why is all this to be swept away?" Newgate was first used on 3d December 1783, when 10 men were executed. From this time the cart process was replaced by a new arrangement. The prisoner was placed on a platform, the rope adjusted, and the platform by the drawing of a bolt suddenly fell in from under him, leaving him to hang by his neck and die by strangulation. If, as sometimes happened, his weight was not sufficient to ensure this, the hangman or even the spectators added their own weight. The Governor concluded the proceedings with a breakfast to certain officials and persons of distinction, whose curiosity had led to their being invited to view the proceedings.

The executioner was formerly sworn in to do his duty, but the office does not appear to have been in England a permanent post. It was held in such disrepute that very often some criminal had to be engaged to fill it. The hangman was not allowed to enter the gaol even to receive his wage, but was paid over the gates, the "toilette" or pinioning being performed by the "yeomen of the halter."

The duty of carrying out the sentence devolving on the sheriff, it rests with him to find the operator, and, in modern times at all events, the same man has been generally employed by all sheriffs. Calcraft, who was usually employed up till 1874, was paid by the Corporation of London £1 : 1s. per week as a retaining-fee, and an extra guinea for each execution. He had 2s. 6d. for each flogging he carried out, and an allowance for "cats" and birch rods. He also had from the county of Surrey £5 : 5s. retaining-fee, and £1 : 1s. for each execution, and £10 for an execution in the country.

The proceedings at an execution are now regulated by an Act passed in 1868, under which executions ceased to be carried out in public. It was decided after full consideration that the scenes at a public execution were so demoralising that they could no longer be tolerated; they collected all the scum of the neighbourhood, and were little less disgusting than the former practice of the procession to the distant place of execution, while the deterrent effects were certainly no greater. From that time, then, they have been carried out inside the gaol, the persons bound to be present are the sheriff, the governor, the chaplain, the doctor, and such other prison officers as the sheriff requires, and any magistrates for the jurisdiction the prisoner belongs to, any one of the prisoner's relations, or such other persons, as the sheriff or (the visiting justices, the latter now replaced by) the Commissioners of Prisons, think proper to admit, may also be present. The Commissioners of Prisons have decided to leave this privilege to the sheriff alone. After the execution a coroner's inquest is held on the body to establish for the public satisfaction that the person sentenced has certainly been hanged, and certain persons have to sign a certificate to this effect. The certificates, etc., have to be exhibited for twenty-four hours at least near the entrance of the prison. The Secretary of State is empowered to make rules to be observed at the execution, both to guard against abuse, give greater solemnity, and for notifying outside that the execution is taking place. The following are the rules made accordingly in August 1868:—

1. For the sake of uniformity it is recommended that executions should take place at the hour of 8 A.M. on the first Monday after the intervention of three Sundays from the day on which sentence is passed.
2. The mode of execution, and the ceremonial attending it, to be the same as heretofore in use.
3. A black flag to be hoisted at the moment of execution, upon a staff placed on an elevated and conspicuous part of the prison, and to remain displayed for one hour.
4. The bell of the prison, or if arrangements can be made for that purpose, the bell of the parish or other neighbouring church, to be tolled for fifteen minutes before and fifteen minutes after the execution.

The actual mode by which death is brought about in the operation of hanging is one of much practical importance, in consideration of the universal feeling, that all painful scenes and all unnecessary and prolonged pain to the criminal should be avoided. Death by hanging may result from contraction of the wind-pipe producing suffocation, or of the blood-vessels producing apoplexy, or by rupture of the spinal cord which produces instant death, even if the necessarily accompanying shock to the nervous system does not do so. It is perhaps difficult to determine which of these is accompanied by the smallest amount of pain, but the latter is no doubt quickest in effect, and so the least horrible to those who are obliged to be spectators. It is effected by a proper adjustment of the rope, and by a sufficient length of drop so proportioned to the weight of the body as to give such momentum as will rupture the ligatures of the spine, and the increase in length of drop is the difference which makes the change between the mode generally adopted up till 1874 and since. This system is not without its dangers, for the rope may break, or the criminal may suffer the torture of having his flesh torn by the strain, so that the precise length of the necessary drop has become a subject of scientific calculations as well as of practical experience.

The practice of exposing the bodies of murderers and others in chains, as a terror and example, commonly prevailed at one period, and was legally authorised in 1832, though it had then ceased to be ordinarily followed.

By a law passed in the reign of Henry VIII. some bodies of murderers were given over for anatomical purposes, and in 1829 this course, which also had been very usual, was prescribed for all. Instances occurred of this proceeding being followed by the resuscitation of the body. In 1832 these laws were superseded by one directing that the bodies should be buried within the precincts of the gaol, the course prescribed also by the Act of 1868 above referred to.

In former days the signature of the king in council on the death-warrant was, so far as the jurisdiction of the Central Criminal Court extends, necessary to justify the sheriff in carrying it into execution, but on the Queen's accession it was thought proper to relieve her, by Act of Parliament, from a duty so painful to any woman, and to a young girl, as Her Majesty then was, so impossible. Her Majesty succeeded to the throne on the 20th June, and on the 17th July an Act was passed to assimilate the practice of the Central Criminal Court to that of other courts in England and Wales in this respect. It enacts that in future no report to Her Majesty shall be necessary in capital cases, and directs that the judge shall order the place and time of execution, not being more than twenty-one days nor less than seven from the date of the order.

A very remarkable circumstance occurred in 1872 in connection with this subject which illustrates the unnoticed survival of various anomalies among us. The Isle of Man is a separate kingdom, and the laws of Great Britain are not of necessity the laws of that little island, for they are framed by the Court of Tynwald. One of the laws passed in 1817 requires the king's warrant to the lieutenant-governor for an execution, and the omission to provide for this case escaped notice until 1872, when a wretched man joined his mother in a petty quarrel with his father, of seventy years of age, about a small property. After going to law they compromised the matter, and the father was to receive a cow from the son, but before this was carried out the son went to the father's cottage and killed him with a pitchfork. The man was sentenced to be hanged, and Her Majesty was called upon to approve the sentence, which, it is needless to say, her strong sense of duty and regard for the constitution enabled her to do, under the advice of the Home Secretary, but, as it will be correctly imagined, with much strain on her feelings.

A sentence of death passed by court martial in the

United Kingdom can only be put in execution with the express sanction of the Crown, which must approve the sentence of every General Court Martial, by which alone a sentence of death can be passed. The Crown has power, however, to assign to some other authority the power of approving sentences by General Courts Martial.

There are people who object to the principle of capital punishment on various grounds, and who sometimes deny its efficiency as a deterrent. When the capital sentence was very common, and when those who suffered were paraded through the town as heroes, and still more when it was common that such a sentence was passed and not carried into effect, it might be natural that it should fail in its effect, but when not weakened by these defects of practice, it can hardly be doubted that a possible murderer is often restrained by the thought of the probable consequences of his contemplated crime. It is not often that one can get at the mind of such a person, or hear the reflections which pass among the criminal classes in the freedom of private intercourse, but chance brought to light on one occasion of late years the workings of the minds of men of this class. A convict in prison in Western Australia found means of surreptitiously passing out a letter to a friend in England. When the letter arrived the friend, for reasons which may be surmised, was not to be found at the address given. It therefore came in the usual course to the dead letter office; thence, in due course, it was returned to the authorities of the prison in which it had been written, and was duly examined and reported. It was found that the writer was informing his friend that in the colony there was a law which made a murderous assault on a warder a capital offence, and he commented on the fact in his own words thus: "They top (*i.e.* hang) a cove out here for slogging (*i.e.* striking) a bloke (*i.e.* a warder). *That bit of rope dear Jack is a great check on a man's temper.*" It would be difficult after this to dispute the deterrent effect of the fear of this punishment.

## CHAPTER III.

### GAOLS IN FORMER TIMES.

SIR JAMES STEPHEN thinks that imprisonment was not mentioned in Anglo-Saxon laws as a punishment, though it was referred to as a way of securing a person who could not give surety. Although it became a common law as well as a statutory punishment, yet gaols were no doubt formerly used more as places of security than of punishment.

The Assizes of Clarendon (1166) and Northampton (1176) provide for the apprehension of criminals, for their safe custody before trial, and for their punishment when found guilty. It appears, however, that difficulties arose from the fact that some counties possessed no gaol or "prisoners' cage," and the deficiency had to be made good at the king's expense. These cages were to be constructed within the king's castles in fortified towns, and there their successors remain to this day at York, Lancaster, Cambridge, Oxford, Chester, Norwich, or on their site, as at Newgate. Under the common law all gaols belonged to the king, and by 5 Henry IV. cap. 10 it was enacted that none should be imprisoned by any Justice of the Peace, but only in the common gaol, saving the franchise of those who had gaols. These franchises embraced very extensive powers of criminal jurisdiction, in some cases even that of life and death. The town of Halifax is said to have exercised this power up to 1650, using an instrument of execution like a guillotine. The Manor Court is said to be a survival of a time when a baron possessed a prison into which he could throw "handhaving and backbearing thieves before he hanged them." The common gaols were under the control of the Sheriff, but the franchise prisons, owned by great noblemen and ecclesiastics, were no doubt managed by them, and those of towns and liberties, who were allowed by their charters to have prisons but had no sheriffs, by the governing bodies of such towns, etc.

A curious relic of these customs existed till quite recently, Lord Bristol claiming till 1877 the appointment of the gaoler at Bury, as being vested in him and not in the Justices.

In the time of Edward VI. and Queen Elizabeth bridewells and houses of correction were instituted, at first rather as hospitals or charities than for actual punishment, but very soon as places of confinement for vagabonds, harlots, and idle persons. By James I. cap. 4 it was enacted that one of these establishments should be provided in every county, and the Justices under whose management it was placed were directed "to provide mills, turns, cards, and such like instruments for setting idle people to work."

Gradually the practice became established (by 1715) of committing criminals of all classes to those houses of correction, and the general system of punishment by imprisonment grew up; but the use of houses of correction for all classes of criminals was not legal till made so by 6 Geo. I. cap. 19. This union was carried to further completion by 5 & 6 Will. IV. cap. 38, under which even sentences of death might be carried out in them; but still the difference in the origin of the two classes of establishments was marked by the distinctions that debtors could be committed only to the gaol, while vagrants could not be committed to the gaol but only to the house of correction. Common sense again went in advance of the law, and united the two buildings under one roof, and placed them both under the same governing staff, but further it could not go, for the law made the gaol under the jurisdiction of the Sheriff, and the house of correction under that of the Justices.

But besides imprisonment, there was, from the time of Charles II., transportation, and all those systems of punishment which grew out of it, and this punishment, by reason of circumstances which will be described, has followed a course quite distinct from the other, and in buildings or establishments specially legalised for this purpose, thus forming a third species of prison in addition to the common gaol and house of correction, so that a description of this portion of our present penal system must be divided into two parts, corresponding to the two divisions into which it has been separated by the history of events, and by the laws passed to provide for circumstances as they have developed.

Imprisonment "with hard labour" was introduced by statute, 16 Geo. III. cap. 43, as an alternative to transportation. The practice of punishing by imprisonment having become established, the necessity of conducting it under some kind of system, and subject to such supervision as should prevent cruelty or abuses arising from ignorance or evil motives, became gradually apparent, though it took a good deal more than a century to force itself so completely into the public mind as to establish the standard of human treatment and high sanitary condition now required in prisons.

The condition of prisons in former times is of interest and importance now as showing what our present laws and system have redeemed us from; and unpopular though it may be to throw any doubt on the sufficiency and the perfection of local management, it is an incontestable fact that it has only been by interfering with, compelling, and overruling the administration of local bodies that these grievous evils have been at length redressed. Nor should there be any surprise at this, for a number of small disunited bodies of various degrees of enlightenment are not likely all to attain of themselves to the highest standard of knowledge or high feeling, and the advanced condition of some few localities coincidently with a very imperfect condition among very many, show that something more than the mere example which is given by one local body to another is necessary to bring about the adoption of the best and most perfect methods of administration of affairs committed to their management. The feeling which gave force to the dislike of the gradual supersession of the local authorities by the Central Government in the administration of prisons is the counterpart of that which led the local justices to resist the intrusion of the King's judges in the early days of the consolidation of the kingdom under the Plantagenets, who, setting themselves to suppress crime and improve the administration of the law, ordained the system under which judges periodically perambulate the country to hold assizes and deliver the gaols. These circuits were held at first at intervals of two and three years, but the local opposition so far prevailed at one time as to exclude them from every county for seven years at a time.

The advantages of local government are indeed obvious, and most of the disadvantages alleged against it arise from the local area being too small, or from confusing local management with amateur and inexperienced management. On all such matters it is a question for consideration whether the advantages of increased efficiency, which should come from the transfer of management to persons with wider experience—from the stronger current of life which is created by uniting small bodies with larger ones, and from the uniformity which cannot be attained by the action of numerous independent bodies, are so great as to counterbalance the educating process which the smaller local bodies or individuals gain from employing themselves in managing these affairs, and the interest or contentment which is sometimes secured by putting such matters into the hands of persons individually known in their localities. The wise solution of the problem is no doubt to combine the two where it is possible, and we shall see further on how this has been effected in regard to the prisons.

Those who desire to obtain an adequate idea of the state our prisons were in "up to a time within the memory of men still living" may read the reports of the societies which laboured for their reform, and those of the inspectors finally appointed, and Major Griffiths' full volumes of the *Chronicles of Newgate*, which contain a mass of research relating to prisons generally, from which I have gathered some very interesting and useful extracts. The following summary will suffice for present purposes.

The rules and administration of the prison depended almost entirely on the gaoler. He was appointed by the proprietor of the prison, and had the right of claiming certain fees from the prisoners for their maintenance and for the enjoyment of certain privileges or exemptions; and the payment of these fees, sometimes exorbitant, was secured to him by the right, frequently exercised, to detain the prisoner after the Court of Law had ordered his discharge.

As these fees varied according to the accommodation, and as certain exemptions could be purchased by them, they formed a source of emolument sufficient to justify the gaoler, according to the principles of the time, in purchasing his place from the proprietor of the gaol. The keeper of the Duke of Portland's prison paid him eighteen guineas per annum for a prison which consisted of one room with cellar under it, which Howard recorded had, at his visit, not been cleaned for months, nor had the prison door been open for weeks.

This principle was considered so natural and regular that in the reign of Queen Elizabeth (1561) the office of Warden of the Fleet was granted as an emolument to Sir Jeremy Whitshed and his heirs for ever. Afterwards the patent was repealed, and one Higgins got the office "by giving £5000 to the late Lord Chancellor Clarendon," and he ultimately sold it to Messrs. Bambridge and

Corbett for £5000. The income of the Warden of the Marshalsea debtors' prison was £3000 to £4000 a year, derived from fees and charges to debtors for necessaries. The presentation to this office was bought up by the Crown by 27 Geo. II. for £10,500. The income of the Warden of the Fleet was £2372 from similar sources. A fee at entrance called garnish, amounting to £1 : 1s. for debtors, 10s. 6d. in Newgate for criminals, was supposed to provide coals, candles, brooms, etc. ; another fee was paid at discharge. In Newgate the fee for a prisoner who desired to be placed on the "State" side was £3 : 3s., and 10s. 6d. a week for a bed. Thirty guineas a week was known to be charged for accommodation in the gaoler's house. The cruelties leading even to murder, which the above-mentioned Bambridge and Corbett practised on the prisoners in order to make the bargain pay, led to an inquiry by a Committee of the House of Commons, and to the more full exposing of the iniquities of the system in seven trials for murder and one for theft, which were instituted in 1730 in consequence against the Keepers of the Fleet and Marshalsea; also to an Act of Parliament to remedy them in 1729, which, however, seems to have largely failed in its object.

Gaolers' fees were abolished by law in 1774, and it was ordered that they were to be paid by salary, but the Act continued to be evaded for some time in this respect, as it seems it was necessary again to abolish them by Act of Parliament in 1813. The transportation Acts sanctioned that which was in principle the foundation of the evil by practically selling the prisoners sentenced to that punishment to the contractors, who undertook to remove them to America or elsewhere, while the Justices, who up to 1783 carried into effect the Hulks' Act, under which the hulks were placed in charge of an overseer, acted on similar principles then, and long after, for they allowed the overseers to be the contractors for the supply of the necessaries for the prisoners in them.

The governors of the local gaols having to make their income out of the prisoners naturally desired to limit their expenditures in assistants, and, therefore, appointed prisoners as "wardsmen" in charge of the others; moreover, these wardsmen bought their places of the gaoler, and they were therefore given not to the most fit, but to the highest bidder.

In order to extract money from the prisoners, the practice was to iron them heavily unless they paid for lighter irons, or for their entire removal—some of them being so heavy that walking, and even lying down to sleep, was difficult and painful. Those who could pay for it were allowed superior accommodation to that which was given to those who could not—and at Newgate it was said, even so late as 1836, by the Inspector, that the inability to pay the ward dues exacted for better accommodation consigned many petty offenders to the place where they unavoidably met with further contamination from the society of the most abandoned and incorrigible inmates of the gaol. All these matters were regulated by the prisoner wardsman.

The issues of food entrusted to the wardsman offered further opportunities of extortion or bribery, for it was issued in the lump, and either scrambled for or might be unfairly divided. The wardsmen, too, had the privilege of selling tea, coffee, sugar, beer, and tobacco,—they charged a fee for the use of knives, forks, and plates, and easily found means to harass those who did not give in to their extortions. They were made, for instance, to wash and swab the floors, forbidden to pass a chalked line on the floor, and so debarred from the fire to warm or cook by, and made subject to a multitude of petty rules invented to annoy them. The privilege of keeping a tap in the prison was also one of the sources of the gaolers' emoluments, and, as unlimited drinking was allowed, the scenes of drunkenness and debauchery may be imagined.

Unrestricted freedom of communication between prisoners was permitted—males and females were mixed together—and the prisoners' families and friends, including burglars and prostitutes, were admitted to pass the day among them; not only did these add to the scenes of debauchery in the prison, but gambling was carried on, burglaries were planned, money coined, and notes forged, inside the prison. It has even been alleged that prisoners were let out at night to rob for the profit of the gaoler, and the gaol was a receptacle for stolen goods. Those who could read might enjoy the flash literature brought in by those purveying newspapers, who sold tobacco at the same time. Swearing and bad language was of course common, and fighting, even to the extent of inflicting great bodily injuries — while leap-frog and fly-the-garter were the more innocent occupations of the prisoners.

The women, who, like the rest, were under the control of male officers only, sat about on the stones of the yard at Newgate, "squalid in attire, ferocious in aspect, begging, swearing, fighting, singing and gaming, dancing and dressing up in men's clothes, so that their ward came to be described as 'Hell upon earth.'"

Even in chapel the prisoners were not made to behave with decency, but talked and greeted each other aloud, and the chaplain, even if desirous to fulfil his duties, found it to be impossible. Supervision in the daytime being thus absent or ineffective, at night matters became worse, and the officers were in fact afraid to visit during these hours, in spite of orders that they should do so. To maintain some kind of discipline, certain prisoners were armed with "a flexible weapon," and Hogarth's prints exhibit the gaoler threatening poor "Kate Hackabout" in her fine clothes with a stick. Disorderly prisoners were chained down to ring bolts, or prisoners were even chained down to rings and bolts to make up for the insecurity of the prison. Even in 1823 prisoners for assize in one gaol were double ironed on first reception, the irons weighing nearly ten to fourteen lbs., and thus fettered at night, they were chained down in bed, the chain being fastened to the floor and to the leg fetters of the prisoners. This lasted from 7 P.M. till 6 A.M., and for six months or more an innocent person might suffer this treatment, for there were but two gaol deliveries in the year. Howard found in the Bishop of Ely's prison prisoners chained down on their backs to the floor, across which were several iron bars, with an iron collar with spikes about their necks, and a heavy iron bar on their legs. This being reported to the king, he "was much affected, and ordered immediate inquiry and redress." To enable the reader to appreciate these facts, it may be stated that at the present time the heaviest irons which can be used weigh only six lbs., and these cannot be applied except in very special cases of necessity.

The common practice of ironing prisoners was justified not only on grounds of security, but as the only means by which prisoners could be distinguished from visitors, and prevented from leaving with them when they were turned out of the prison at night.

The diet of the criminal prisoners was wretched in the extreme, except for those who could pay for something better than was given to those without means,—"bread boiled in water, a pennyworth of bread per diem," a fourpenny loaf, and so on. Criminal prisoners in the common gaol were originally dependent on charity, but from the time of Elizabeth they were maintained by a small allowance of 1d. or 2d. a day from the county, or seven or eight ounces of bread. Prisoners sentenced by the Judges to transportation were entitled to 2s. 6d. a week from the Exchequer, but not those sentenced by Quarter Sessions.

Those in bridewells were supposed to maintain themselves by their work, but, as no means of working were provided, they depended on charity or starved. Debtors were dependent entirely on charitable gifts and bequests, many of which remain to this day, and they were worse off than the felons, though by law the creditor who incarcerated his debtor should have furnished 4d. per diem for his maintenance. A box hung outside the prison to receive the gifts of the benevolent, and in Exeter the prisoners were marched about the streets soliciting charity, the produce of which they were, as Howard relates, once robbed of by their keeper. The charitable doles were supplemented by food seized as improper for sale, light weight, etc. In short, they were insufficiently supplied with water, air, and light, and many of the visitors who thronged and crowded the gaol came to bring food and necessaries to their friends.

As to the clothing worn by the prisoners, it is described as ragged, squalid, and filthy, they were seen with no stockings and no soles to their shoes, even in the depth of winter; their bedding consisted of a couple of ragged rugs, and they lay on stone or oak floors; when the prisons came to be densely crowded, each prisoner was allowed a width of eighteen inches to sleep in, and the floor was frequently covered. Cleanliness was, of course, absolutely neglected—a pump in the yard was the only means of washing supplied, under which those prisoners were forced whom their fellows found intolerably offensive even to them.

The wretched state of the buildings—their unfitness for their purpose, and the overcrowding which occurred in them—lay at the root of much of the evil condition of the prisoner, and reform in this matter was the first essential to any improvement. In 1755 the Common Council of London said that the prison in Newgate was habitually overcrowded with victims of public justice under the complicated distresses of poverty, nastiness, and disease; neither water, air, nor light being furnished in sufficient quantities. The prisons are described as not water-tight, the windows not repaired—they had no glass, only oiled paper. Nevertheless, in 1785 the population of Newgate Prison amounted to nearly 600; in 1801 there were 275 debtors and 375 felons; while in 1802 there were 720; in 1813 there were 340 on the debtor's side, built for 100; in the female felons' ward 120 in the space which was intended for, but probably inadequate for, 60; and later on it is said as many as 1200 prisoners were lodged within the space of three-fourths of an acre. The overcrowding was partly due to the delay in removing prisoners sentenced to be transported. In Bristol Prison in 1818 was a vault in which prisoners were confined level with the river and very damp. The smell was something more than can be expressed by the word "disgusting." The only ventilation of this "dark, cheerless, damp, unwholesome cavern" was by a kind of chimney, which the prisoners stuffed up, and which the turnkey had never known to be opened. Kidderminster gaol consisted of one damp cold room, into which air could gain admission only through a grating level with the street. This grating was also used by the friends of prisoners to carry drink to them through quills or reeds.

But worst of all was the moral contamination which resulted from the necessarily close unregulated association in which the prisoners, innocent and guilty, corrupt and hardened, male and female, sick and well, were herded together; and, besides the dreadful overcrowding, the other unwholesome sanitary conditions of prison life. We read of an unfortunate man of the law having to sleep between a highwayman and a murderer; and the poor man, who could not fall in with the ways of his associates, being harassed by false charges, and brought up before a mock judge who sentenced him to the "pillory," *i.e.* tied with a chain about his neck. Even the mistaken ideas of kindness increased these evils, for not only were crowds of visitors allowed, as already described, but the debtors, who made up the larger part of the population, were allowed to have their families in with them, and they of course consorted with the felons.

The results of this condition of things in the propagation of moral disease was not to the eyes of those days at all apparent, but the physical disease was impressed on them from time to time in a manner which should have awakened attention if medical science and humanity had not both been on a low level.

The gaol fever, as typhus was then called,—the inevitable consequence of the overcrowding, misery, and neglect of all sanitary requirements which characterised the prisons,—was known to have prevailed from 1414. It is described as a contagious, putrid, very pestilential fever, with tremblings, twitchings, restlessness, delirium, and sometimes frenzy or lethargy; and with livid pustules and purple spots.

At the Black Assizes at Oxford in 1577 the Lord Chief Baron, the sheriff, and 300 more died within forty hours from the fearful disease communicated to the court by the prisoners brought up for trial before it —the disease spreading into the city and neighbourhood caused many more deaths. Several other occasions are on record when similar results followed; and Lord Bacon calls "the smell of the gaol the most pernicious infection next to the plague. When prisoners have been long and close and nastily kept, whereof we have had in our times experience twice or thrice, both judges that sat upon the trial, and numbers of them that attended the business or were present, sickened upon it or died."

But though the cause was thus clearly known and capable of remedy—"prisoners long and close and nastily kept"—the disease was still allowed to originate those fearful calamities, and no doubt to kill multitudes in the prisons whose death created no sensation or even notice. In 1730 at Taunton some prisoners brought from Ilchester gaol for trial infected the court, and the Lord Chief Baron, the sergeant, the sheriff and some hundreds besides, died of the gaol distemper. In London, in May 1750, 100 persons awaiting trial were crowded mostly into two rooms 14 by 7 by 7 feet high, besides some in the bail dock—many had long been confined in the foul wards of Newgate. The court itself was only 30 feet square and crowded, and from the dock and rooms beyond an open window carried the infection across the court to the bench. The Lord Mayor, an alderman, and two judges, speedily died, and forty more, including under-sheriffs, bar, and jury, fell victims. It may naturally be supposed that the results of this terrible malady were not confined even to the neighbourhood of the courts and gaols where it originated or first showed itself. It was the practice in these days to pardon criminals on condition of their enlisting in the army, or serving in the navy; and distant bodies of troops were infected either by these recruits or by the escorts bringing back soldiers temporarily in prison. The first English fleet sent to America lost by it above 2000 men.

The Acts of Elizabeth and James I. already referred to seem to have been the first which recognised the advantages of requiring prisoners to perform some work instead of passing their time in idleness; and in the

19th year of Charles II. was passed an Act which enjoined justices to provide prisoners with work.

The Parliaments of the last century, impressed with the increase of crime and other considerations, passed a considerable number of Acts intended to prevent the mischief arising from having no employment in prison; to ensure the proper construction of prisons with a view to separating classes of prisoners, who would suffer morally by close communication; and to prevent the dreadful epidemics and ill health which a bad sanitary condition entailed not only on the inmates but on others who were brought in contact with them. The Act 14 Geo. III. cap. 59 contains clear regulations to prevent overcrowding and ensure cleanliness in order to guard against the gaol fever, and the justices were ordered to provide sufficient space, including an infirmary, and to have the walls of each room scraped and whitewashed every year; but these injunctions were disregarded. Some Acts of the same tenor had been passed in the previous century, but without much result; and though various philanthropists endeavoured through the seventeenth and eighteenth centuries to promote improvements in prison management, among whom Howard stands out prominently as the chief apostle of prison reform, the effect had been confined to some few localities where the local magistrates were more than usually enlightened, such as in Sussex in 1785 under the guidance of the Duke of Richmond, and in Gloucestershire from 1783 under Sir G. O. Paul, who established a system which nearly approached the best we have now arrived at in spite of the difficulties he encountered from the immobility of his brother magistrates; but all his arrangements and improvements were by 1819 swamped in the deluge of crime which characterised the early part of this century, which was due, in part at least, to bad criminal laws, and bad poor laws badly administered.

In 1778 an Act of Parliament approved the adoption of solitary imprisonment, with labour and instruction, which, it affirmed, would deter and reform better than transportation, and this Act prescribed the size of cells, which were to be not less than 10 by 7 by 9.

In 1784 an Act was passed providing that prison regulations should be passed for general guidance, and that prisoners should be classified as follows, and kept quite separate:—(1) Convicted felons; (2) persons charged with or suspected of felony; (3) convicted misdemeanants; (4) persons charged with or suspected of misdemeanour; (5) debtors; and that in each of these classes males should be quite distinct from females.

Howard found that the justices did not care to do more than look at the outside of the gaol, and that the sheriff only cared for the safe custody of the prisoners; and he urged, among other important suggestions, that the magistrates should take some interest in their prison, and should visit, inspect, and supervise it in turns to detect and prevent abuses, and to institute a good system of administration. In 1791 an Act was passed enjoining justices to visit and inspect their prison three times every quarter, and to report in writing to the Quarter Sessions on its state.

In 1814 the appointment of chaplains was made compulsory.

In 1813 prison reform had the great advantage of

being taken up by some members of the Society of Friends, and through them of the united support of an energetic, wealthy, and philanthropic body. In 1817 was formed the Society for the Improvement of Prison Discipline, which had several "Friends" among its leading members. Its reports record that in 1818 there were 518 prisons in the United Kingdom, to which more than 100,000 prisoners were committed in the year, and that only 23 of these had been subdivided as required by the 24 Geo. III. cap. 54. The Society reported that 59 prisons had no division between males and females, 136 had only one division for this purpose, 68 had only two, etc. In 445 prisons no employment of any kind was provided. The overcrowding was excessive in 100 gaols; in the space for 8545 there had been crowded 13,057. In Newgate the accumulation of prisoners awaiting transportation had amounted in 1785 to 600 persons.

The labour and influence of Mrs. Fry should be recorded in any account, however brief, of the course of prison reform. It was in 1813 that she first visited Newgate and saw the terrible condition of the female prisoners as clearly described, and "the abandoned wickedness which everything bespoke." "The begging, gaming, fighting, singing, dancing, and dressing up in men's clothes, in 'Hell above ground.'" By personal intercourse and visitation she formed these wretched women into classes, tamed, instructed, and humanised them, got them to work, induced them to adopt rules, and enlisted them on the side of order, and effected results so extraordinary as to render a visit to the female department of Newgate one of the fashionable sensations of the day.

This result was of more than questionable advantage, and when it came to such a point that at the religious services held by the ladies there were twenty-three visitors, many of them gentlemen, to twenty-eight prisoners, it could not be doubted that there must be a considerable admixture of bad effect as well as good on the prisoners. The irregular authority which had been necessarily conferred on the ladies in order that they might be able to carry out their reforms, which would never have been effected but for their volunteer zeal, faith, and self-sacrifice, became a source of difficulty so soon as the regular authorities in the prison had been stimulated to do their duty, and shown how to set about it, and, in fine, the common experience was repeated,—the successors of the first apostles of this movement, their equals, perhaps, in zeal, sentiment, and humanity, were not their equals in judgment, and were not recognised as having the same claims to attention as those who had worked the original miracle. Until this time arrived, however, there was ample scope for the labour of all the force of the prison reformers.

In 1823-24 were passed the important gaol Acts—4 Geo. IV. cap. 64 and 5 Geo. IV. cap. 85. These Acts proposed to provide not only for the safe custody and punishment, but for the preservation of the health, and improvement of the morals of the inmates; it enforced the employment of all, including "hard labour" for some, provided that males and females should be absolutely separate, that the classification of prisoners before referred to should be carried out, that female prisoners should be under female officers, and that there should be daily religious services and instruction by schoolmasters in reading and writing. The use of irons except in urgent necessity was forbidden, and every prisoner was to sleep separately, if possible in a separate cell.

The Prison Discipline Society kept the subject constantly in view, and little by little the local authorities aroused themselves to the necessity for adopting the improvements enjoined by the Act, but the provision of separate sleeping cells, and even of sufficient associated accommodation, was still, for the most part, neglected, and bedding and clothing still denied in some prisons. The rules and practices in the different prisons still varied excessively; even the hours of labour were in one prison seven, and in another ten and a half. The use of the tread-wheel became very general, and even females were in some cases made to drive it.

The diet, of course, varied; in some bread alone was given; in others, meat, soup, gruel, and beer; in some a money allowance was paid; and in some cases the diet given could be supplemented by the earnings of the prisoners, of which they had at their own disposal a proportion which varied at each prison.

The Act was not made to apply to the gaols of the smallest local jurisdictions, which most needed reform, because Mr. Peel, who introduced it, hoped that they would themselves adopt the only possible reform which could be effectual, namely, to sweep their gaols away and combine with some larger body. This was naturally a slow process, for there were 170 boroughs, cities, towns, and liberties having criminal jurisdiction, and 160 of them had prisons, most of which were in a terribly bad condition.

By 1835 the unwearied exertions of prison reformers

whose statements were sifted and substantiated by a Committee of the House of Commons in 1831, and of the House of Lords in 1835, had so far educated the public mind as to cause the Government to pass an Act 5 & 6 Will. IV. cap. 38, framed largely on the recommendations of the latter.

The House of Lords' Committee had pointed out the truth, which seems so obvious as not to need demonstration, that a sentence of imprisonment should be carried out uniformly wherever it might happen that the criminal was confined, and to this end that the rules of prisons should be subject to the approval of the Secretary of State,—an important alteration, for they had hitherto been considered to be the province of the judges of assize; that the prisoners should be furnished by the authorities with a suitable diet, to be approved by the Secretary of State, and should have no other food; that they should not be furnished with money for any purpose; that tobacco should be forbidden "as a stimulating luxury, inconsistent with any notion of strict discipline, and the due pressure of just punishment"; that prison officers should have no profit from prisoners' earnings; that letters and visits to prisoners should be allowed only under restriction and limitations; that religious and literary instruction should be insisted on; that the power of prisoners employed in positions of trust should be controlled and limited; and, above all, that the system of classification hitherto enforced should be replaced by the entire separation of prisoners, except during divine service, labour, or instruction, as the best means of preventing contamination and ensuring proper discipline. On their recommendation there were appointed Inspectors of Prisons (a security which had been urged without effect at least a century before) for the purpose of ensuring the fulfilment of the requirements of the law on various points relating to the treatment of prisoners and prison discipline. These inspectors, of whom there might be five for Great Britain, had power to visit all prisons, to inquire into all matters therein, and to report annually to the Secretary of State. A uniform code of rules and a uniform diet were drawn up by a committee of inspectors under the Under-Secretary of State, circulated by authority of Sir James Graham, and finally adopted.

This Act was followed in a few years by another passed in 1839—2 & 3 Vict. cap. 56—which gave the Secretary of State certain power over the designs of new prisons or the alteration of old ones; and though this Act did not compel, it permitted the confinement of each prisoner in a separate cell, and left the justices to adopt this or an improved system of classified association. It provided that where separate cells were adopted they should be certified fit for use in all respects, and ensured that on this most important department of prison management, which is so vitally connected with security, health, morality, discipline, and economical administration, the prisons should be constructed on the best plans and with the most perfect details which experience could devise. To aid the Secretary of State, and to advise the local authorities in these matters, a further Act passed in 1845—7 & 8 Vict. cap. 50—authorised the appointment of an officer under the name of Surveyor-General of Prisons, to whom all plans of proposed prisons, or alterations of old ones (including police cells), are referred.

The important part which prison construction plays in the creation of a good prison system will be evident to any person who visits prisons in certain foreign countries, where prisoners are still herded together night and day, where cleanliness, order, and supervision are almost impossible, where foul odours from neglect of sanitary conditions meet one at every turn, and where ventilation is as little regarded as in that prison (the Borough Compton) in which the turnkey avowed that "the smell on opening the door was enough to knock down a horse." This very condition the present writer experienced in visiting a military prison abroad in company with the general commanding in the province, and it was curious as an illustration of the way in which such conditions come to be accepted as part of the natural order of things, that this high functionary undauntedly walked into a dark cell in which a soldier had been locked up for a long period, and from which on opening the door there proceeded such a stifling, foul, and peculiar smell as might fairly be described in the language of the English turnkey in 1818.

As a corollary of the Act of 1839 the Government determined to construct a model prison, which should be an example both of construction and discipline to the whole country, and this was carried into effect by the building of Pentonville Prison, under the supervision of Mr. Crawford, Mr. Whitworth Russell, the two first inspectors, both very prominent prison reformers, and Captain, afterwards Sir Joshua, Jebb, R.E.

In this prison, commenced in 1840 and opened in

December 1842, each inmate was furnished with a separate cell lighted by a window looking into a spacious court, and supplied with fresh air (warmed when necessary by passing through channels heated by hot-water pipes), which was drawn through by extraction flues in order to keep it pure and wholesome. In sanitary matters the construction was much in advance of the time, and, in fact, was almost up to the present level of sanitary construction.

Facilities for economical and effective control and supervision were created by building these cells in rows and tiers, opening on to galleries round long corridors, the corridors uniting in a central hall, so that the general plan of the prison was radiating.

Pentonville prison at its first construction contained 520 cells, and cost £90,000, or £180 per cell. Its plan and mode of construction have been followed generally in England and in foreign countries as well.

The general design was not the sole invention of the builders of Pentonville, for the radiating plan with separate cells had been adopted in Rome in the beginning of the seventeenth century at San Michele, the virtues of separation in monastic establishments perhaps suggesting its application for taming and reforming prisoners. Mr. Blackburn had about 1789 designed for Howard, who perhaps had seen San Michele, a model prison at Liverpool on the radiating plan, and forty or fifty more were constructed on the same plan in various parts of Great Britain, the relative merits of the circular plan (of which some examples still remain) and the radiating plan having been long a subject of discussion among prison reformers. But the prison which probably was in the minds of the projectors of Pentonville was that at Cherry Hill, Philadelphia, which had been designed by Mr. Haviland with greatly improved arrangements about 1829, and this had been visited and reported on by the Commission which visited the United States in 1834 to glean the result of the experiments which had been carried on in that country in prison construction and prison management.

An interesting chapter might indeed be written on the subject of prison construction and its bearing on health, as well as on other more special considerations, but space will not allow to do more than refer to the principal types which have been adopted.

The point which seems to have been principally in the minds of the designers of the earlier types was to provide for the security of the prisoners by massive construction, and for their supervision by placing the house of the Governor in the middle, the prisoners' cells or rooms being sometimes arranged on a polygon surrounding this house, and connected with it by walls dividing the interior into yards for exercise, or sometimes arranged in blocks radiating from it but not connected with it, and so themselves dividing the space into separate yards. These cell-blocks were never planned, according to the present practice, with a central corridor with galleries on each tier, into which the cells or rooms open—but each floor was completely distinct, and the communications between the floors were frequently tortuous and restricted. As a sample of this, York Prison, which still exists, may be referred to, and also as an example of wasteful construction, for in it, under the influence, as alleged, of the Rev. Sydney

Smith, a prison of most superfluous solidity but of very inferior type in all other respects was built at a cost of £1200 per prisoner. The average expenditure on these gaols was calculated at about £300 per prisoner accommodated. Millbank Prison, which will be hereafter referred to, embodied these principles on a very large scale. In the centre is the chapel; round it are the offices and quarters disposed to form a hexagon; and on each side of this hexagon, as a base, is built a block, of which the general plan forms a pentagon. Each side of the pentagon comprises three tiers of cells, which look into the inner court they surround; and in the centre of the pentagon was a tower from which watch and guard could be kept over the inmates.

The essential feature of the type of prison which finally prevailed, and is now followed wherever there is an effective prison system, is that of assigning a separate cell to each prisoner. This cell the prisoner under a short sentence or during a limited part of a long one occupies at all times, except during divine service, exercise, or instruction, unless he is on the tread-wheel; and during the remainder of a long sentence, at all events at night and during meals, or generally when not employed on regulated and associated labour. This system was not adopted without much discussion and strong opposition from those who thought it too unnatural to be justifiable, and whose ideas derived much support from the results on the mental and nervous condition of some prisoners who had been subjected to it, principally in America, owing to the extreme rigour with which it was enforced. These advocated rather the association of prisoners, a condition which they said was more healthy and natural, made instruction in trades easier, and afforded better industrial results. The mutual contamination, which all agreed was the great evil to be guarded against, they argued, should be prevented by the enforcement of a rule of rigid silence. This condition of things was, however, obviously no less unnatural than the other, and had the additional disadvantage that the irresistible temptation to break or evade the rule of silence could only be met (and that but partially) by constant punishment or the terror of it. It was settled finally that separation could be carried out without any injury to the mental or bodily health, if accompanied by very easy safeguards, that it was more deterrent, afforded greater opportunities for the working of reformatory influences, and if the industrial results were smaller, this was in some measure compensated for by the smaller staff required to maintain order and discipline.

In six years after Pentonville was built fifty-four new prisons were built after its model, affording 11,000 separate cells. Though the results of legislation had been that prisons were considerably improved as compared with those of the early part of the century, there was still very much to be done. The want of the desired uniformity, which implied that very many prisons were still much below the proper standard of efficiency, was by 1850 again forced on the attention of Parliament. The dietaries varied in spite of the advice of the Government—in some they were too liberal, in others too low; the separate cells were often too small—badly ventilated and imperfectly warmed; in some prisons the inmates had one hour's exercise in a day, in others half a day was appropriated to this purpose; the employment of the prisoners differed in all degrees between perpetual penal labour of the tread-wheel type, and the extraordinary crotchet which was carried out at Reading and elsewhere, under which "prisoners were employed in nothing but education," by which was meant literary education. In this prison the inmates learned lessons all day, except when exercising, attending chapel, and cleaning cells, etc. As a privilege they might, "when tired of reading," "pick a little oakum," but this was quite optional, and hard, heavy labour was absolutely forbidden in order that the whole attention might be devoted to literature—the establishment was a criminal university, and acquired the name of the "Read-read-reading Gaol." As a final climax of burlesque absurdity the Bible was made the principal lesson book (in one prison the solitary prisoners were supplied with nothing else whatever), and a reformatory influence was supposed to be achieved by requiring the criminals to commit large portions of the Testament to memory. This result was figured by one irreverent critic to be so effectively achieved that a felon was said to have been so distressed that the end of his sentence interrupted his studies when he had only "got as far as Ephesians," that he came back (under sentence for sheep-stealing) to learn the rest of the Testament.

A select Committee of the House of Commons in 1850 deemed "it their duty to state that several prisons are still in a very unsatisfactory condition, and that proper punishment, separation, or reformation in them is impossible." They recommended that "the Legislature should entrust increased power to some central authority of enforcing uniform adherence to rules laid down by Parliament in respect to construction and discipline, and observed that such increased powers would be best exercised by a Board subject to the authority of the Secretary of State." In this they anticipated by a quarter of a century the legislation of 1877. They recommended the entire separation of all prisoners both before and after trial by day and by night, except during hours of labour, worship, or instruction, and that during such hours effectual means should be taken to prevent intercourse between prisoners. Further, that the separation system carried out at Pentonville, and many county and borough prisons, should be applied continuously to all prisoners under sentences not exceeding three months, not mentally or physically disqualified, and to prisoners under long sentences, but not for a longer period than twelve months, after which they should labour in association, but without intercourse. To carry out this proposal they recommended that district prisons should be created by Government, and intended that thereby longer terms of imprisonment might be substituted for transportation.

The recommendations of this Committee formed the foundation for a distinct advance towards our present system both in regard to short and long sentences.

From 1836 onwards the treatment of those prisoners who were sentenced to transportation aroused much attention, and this branch of the subject must be treated separately. But no further considerable step was taken to improve the ordinary prisons till 1865, when an Act was passed framed on the recommendations of a Committee of the House of Lords, which sat in 1863. Their report commented very strongly on the great difference in the punishment of prisoners and construction of prisons in different localities; the imperfection of construction of some; the absence of light; and of means, for prisoners when locked in, of communicating with the warders; the continuance of pernicious association in many; the complete idleness in some prisons; and the variety, as above detailed, in the employment of prisoners, etc. The Committee recommended that separation should be the rule in all prisons; that penal labour of the tread-wheel type should be enforced, though, if the local justices preferred industrial labour, they should have power to adopt that form during a portion of the sentence. They pointed out, however, that it would be a great mistake to make industrial work for profit the leading consideration. They also recommended, as a means of making the sentence deterrent, that prisoners should endure "hard labour, hard fare, and a hard bed"; that to that end they should during a part of the sentence be deprived of a mattress, and sleep on the bed-board; that dietaries should be more uniform, and more attention given to this subject (in one prison they pointed out that the food was furnished from a neighbouring inn), and the hours of labour better regulated—the necessity of which they illustrated by showing that in one prison the inmates passed fifteen hours in bed.

They condemned the unrestrained association of all classes in minor borough prisons, where the prisoners slept two in a bed in dormitories, which were without light, control, or ventilation, and the warder afraid to enter after dark. Indeed at this period, as well as formerly, the first step towards improvement should have been the closing of many of the minor prisons, for in 1862 there were in England and Wales 193 prisons, of which 63 had on an average only 25 prisoners; 22 had between 11 and 25; 14 had between 11 and 6; and 27 had less than 6. Some even had no inmates at all.

The Prisons Act of 1865 recognised for the first time the truth that, if uniformity was necessary, it must not be left to the option of the local authorities to conform or not, and it therefore enacted a code of rules as part of the statute,—a clumsy expedient adopted to avoid the appearance of superseding local authority by central control, but, in fact, doing it in the most objectionable way. As this Act still regulates our prisons it is necessary to set out the principles which it enforces.

The distinction between a gaol and a house of correction was abolished. The jurisdiction of the sheriff was limited to prisoners under sentence of death. Every prison authority was required to provide a prison containing separate cells for all its prisoners, with separate divisions for females, for debtors, and for misdemeanants "of the first division"—*i.e.* misdemeanants ordered by the Court who tried them to be so classed. This distinction had been introduced by an Act passed in 1840, in which "first-class misdemeanants" were exempted from the provisions of the Gaol Act of 1839. The separate cells were to be such as could be certified by an inspector of prison to be of such a size, and to be lighted, warmed, ventilated, and fitted up in such a manner as may be requisite for health, and furnished with means of enabling the prisoner to communicate at any time with an officer of the prison. A gaoler, a chaplain of the Church of England, surgeon, and female officers for female prisoners, were to be appointed.

Much discussion took place as to the meaning which should be assigned to the phrase "hard labour," which clearly does not explain itself, and was first adopted in Acts of Parliament framed before the days of scientific accuracy of expression. The medical definition of it given at the time we are now treating of was such labour as "visibly quickens the breath and opens the pores"; but this definition, though it probably satisfies one set of ideas on the subject, could not be adopted as the stereotyped mode of enforcing a sentence which could be passed on persons of both sexes, of all conditions and habits of life, and for long periods. The Prisons Act, 1865, therefore adopted the course of enacting that hard labour was to be of two classes, first-class hard labour to be at the tread-wheel, shot-drill, crank, capstan, stone-breaking, and "such other like description of hard body labour." Any other approved kind of labour was called second class, and the prison authority was required to provide means for enforcing hard labour of these two classes. Every male prisoner of sixteen years of age and upwards sentenced to hard labour was required to be kept at first-class hard labour for at least three months during a period of not more than ten nor less than six hours a day. The justices were authorised to make rules which might keep him at this labour for the entire sentence, or they might, after three months, employ him in hard labour of the second class; prisoners under sentence of fourteen days or less might be employed all the time in second-class hard labour if the justices desired. Clearly, in respect to the most important matter of labour and employment, the Act did not fulfil its object of introducing uniformity.

The dietaries were to be framed by the justices, and they were to make rules on any other matters, subject to the approval of the Secretary of State. This, and a rule in the schedule directing them to make rules for the classification of prisoners who are not debtors and not criminal prisoners under the Act, is the only provision for regulating the distinction between the treatment of misdemeanants of the first division and others.

If the justices failed in complying with the Act, the Secretary of State was empowered to stop the contribution made by the Treasury towards the expenses of the gaol, or he might also close an inadequate prison; but as he could not do this unless some other prison authority was willing to receive the prisoners, this power was practically of little use.

Provision was made for the modification of any rule in its application to any prisoner for reasons of health, and generally for the medical care of prisoners and the preservation of their health. A coroner's inquest was to be held on every prisoner who died in the prison, and no person connected with the prison might be on the jury.

Buildings and alterations of prisons were to be carried out subject to the approval of the Secretary of State, and the appointment of Surveyor-General of Prisons, before adverted to, was continued. Facilities and encouragement were afforded to prison authorities to combine their prisons.

Visiting justices were to be appointed by the Quarter

Sessions to supervise the prison on all points under rules laid down for the purpose, and to see that the Act and the rules of the prison were enforced; and they were required to report each quarter to the Quarter Sessions.

Prison authorities were authorised to make a grant to aid a prisoner in finding work on his discharge, so that he might not then find himself subject to the difficulties and temptations which arise from want, necessity, and idleness.

The schedule of the Act comprises a detail of rules for the administration and discipline of the prison; cleanliness, security, and health are provided for; untried prisoners are to be separated from the convicted; spirits and tobacco are forbidden; debtors and untried prisoners are allowed to procure their own food, clothing, and bedding at their own expense; each male prisoner is to sleep in a separate cell, or if special circumstances prevented this yet on no occasion are two to sleep in a cell alone; gaming is forbidden; debtors and untried prisoners may be allowed to work; and the employment of all convicted prisoners is provided for.

Daily prayers, divine service, and religious instruction are also to be provided; and prisoners belonging to various religious persuasions are allowed to receive the ministrations of the ministers thereof. Reading, writing, and arithmetic are to be taught; but this is not to diminish the hours apportioned to labour.

Prisoners are allowed to receive visits from and to communicate with their friends under such rules and restrictions as the prison authorities should lay down.

The power of punishment for prison offences is restricted to the justices and the gaoler—the latter may order an offender to be placed in close confinement for three days on bread and water, the former can order one month in a punishment cell, or a convicted felon sentenced to hard labour may be flogged. Irons or mechanical restraint are only to be used in a case of urgent necessity, and then immediately reported to a visiting justice, and no prisoner may be subject to such restraint for more that twenty-four hours without the written authority of a visiting justice.

No prisoner may be employed in the discipline of the prison or the service of any officer, or in the service or instruction of any other prisoner. The prisoners are to be informed of the rules applicable to them.

Strict rules are laid down to ensure the due performance of his duty by the gaoler, and as to his power over officers under him.

The Act concluded by closing the prisons of thirteen boroughs and one liberty, and repealed the previous Acts inconsistent with or rendered unnecessary by this one.

## CHAPTER IV.

### MODERN PRISONS.

The next great step in the reform of our prison system was the introduction of the Prisons Bill in 1876, and its enactment in 1877. The justification of this measure was that, notwithstanding the Act of 1865, the desired uniformity in the system of punishment had not been secured, while the facilities for locomotion and travel had become so great that the difference between the effect of the sentences in different localities became very apparent, and was said even to be taken into account by the criminal classes. The buildings, moreover, in many cases, remained wofully below the proper standard, and the power of the Secretary of State to require improvements was found inadequate, or, what had the same result, very difficult to enforce. It was obvious, moreover, to those who investigated the matter, that this ineffective system was also unduly costly, and that both defects were due to the impossibility of getting a great number of independent authorities, large and small, to conform in the necessary degree in the details of the system, or to unite their prisons in such a manner as a reasonable regard for economy would have directed. There were still 113 county, borough, and liberty prisons, and these were managed and superintended by about 2000 justices or more. It is obvious that when power and responsibility are shared among so many they become unduly diluted or frittered away; and the supervision exercised by such a large body—who individually could rarely, and collectively never, acquire the detail knowledge which comes only by accumulated practical experience—must, from the nature of things, be very uncertain and imperfect, while a check of this nature is very liable to be delusive.

The possibility of crying abuses and continuous systematic cruelty existing in spite of, and under cover of, such a check was demonstrated by the revelations made in the investigation into Birmingham Borough Gaol in 1850, which forms the foundation of Charles Reade's novel and play, *Never too late to Mend.* Supervision so liable to be delusive in fact lends itself most easily to the establishment and cloaking of abuses, for it relieves those who are likely to commit them of responsibility, and even provides them with defence—the more effective in proportion as the supposed combined checking and managing power resides in persons who are powerful and important, and independent of any superior authority.

It happened that at this moment the Government were desirous of doing something in relief of local taxation, and the assumption of the charge for maintaining the prisons afforded a very favourable opportunity of effecting this object, because it was seen that by diminishing the number of prisons and by other possible measures, the burden from which the localities would be relieved would be much more than would be thrown on the taxes when the service had been reorganised.

But as a natural consequence of transferring to Parliament the duty of providing funds for the maintenance of prisons, it also transferred to the Government the complete control of the prisons, and thus ensured the long-desired uniformity, besides introducing that responsibility for their management which attends our system of Parliamentary Government.

The Prisons Act, 1877, transferred, therefore, the whole of the prison establishments and their contents, except goods manufactured for sale and materials provided for that purpose, to the Government in the person of the Home Secretary. It created a body of Commissioners to be appointed by Royal Warrant to manage the new department, and placed under them a staff of inspectors and of other officers through whom the necessary personal supervision and control over so many distant establishments could be exercised, and by whom those establishments could be administered. The appointment and control of officers, and all the duties and responsibilities involved in this administration of the prisons, was transferred to the Secretary of State and the Commissioners of Prisons.

It may naturally be supposed that a change such as this was not made without much opposition from those who, from various reasons, disapproved of the transfer of management from local bodies to a department of the State, in which, indeed, they but repeated the local opposition already referred to as having centuries before been offered to the supersession of the local justices by the practice of sending judges on circuit to try offenders, and more recently, at the beginning of this century, to placing the hulks in which prisoners sentenced to transportation were confined under Government management instead of under local justices, but, as a matter of fact, the organisation actually adopted, as will be seen, retained for the local authorities very high and important functions, for it placed them in the position of a court of justice, before whom the governor could bring any prisoner, of whose ill conduct he might have to complain to them, and to whom the prisoner could appeal if he desired to complain of any oppression or neglect on the part of the prison officials.

The law as it stood before 1877 placed upon certain bodies, called "Prison Authorities," the duty of providing sufficient prison accommodation, of a certain quality, for the prisoners belonging to their jurisdiction. The prison authorities were defined in the Act of 1865 as those local bodies which by statute, charter, etc., were entitled to maintain prisons, and the Act 1877 made it incumbent on them to hand over to the Home Secretary suitable prison accommodation sufficient in amount.

Sufficient prison accommodation as respects the number of prison cells which the prison authorities had to furnish, was defined as being the average daily number of prisoners maintained by the prison authority during the five years ending 31st December 1876, and each cell was required to be one certified under the Act of 1865 as fulfilling the required conditions.

In default of having such accommodation to hand over, the prison authority was required to pay £120 for every prisoner for whom such accommodation was not handed over.

It was successfully contended during the discussion on the Bill, that as all future prison expenses were to be undertaken by Government, those prison authorities who had, in anticipation of probable increase in the number of prisoners, provided a reasonable amount of accommodation in excess of the average of the maximum numbers of the preceding five years, thus saving expenditure which it was presumed that the Government would have to incur, should receive compensation for the excess which they handed over.

It would not have been unreasonable to wait till this presumption was justified before saddling the country with this expenditure, but the clause was proposed and accepted in Committee on the Bill by a jaded house, and affords a curious little example of our mode of legislation. It resulted in our paying £127,478 for cells built in anticipation of an increase of about 1376 prisoners in the average prison population of the particular localities where this provision was made. If this supposition, therefore, was correct, it was reasonable to expect the average prison population of the whole country to increase by nearly 3000 during the ensuing few years, and if all localities had thus provided in advance, the country would have had to pay a quarter of a million, without any necessity at all, for, as a matter of fact, as will be shown later on, the prison population has continuously and largely decreased.

The sum fixed to clear the local authority of its responsibility in furnishing actual prison accommodation, viz. £120 per cell, was much below what any prison authority would actually have had to pay for providing the accommodation, as the cost of the under-mentioned prisons constructed by the local authorities conclusively demonstrates.

| Prison. | Cost per Cell exclusive of Land. |
|---|---|
| Hull | £198 |
| Manchester | 140 |
| Salford | 140 |
| Birmingham | 157 |
| Winchester | 161 |
| Perth | 150 |
| Lincoln (parts of Lindsey) | 192 |
| Aylesbury | 153 |
| Reading | 197 |
| Wandsworth | 198 |
| Holloway | 209 |

A new prison contemplated at Maidstone was estimated at £185 per cell.

The avowed object of the Act being that the number of prisons should be diminished, and it being obviously probable that from time to time changes would occur which would lead to the abandonment of certain prisons, provision was made for restoring any prison so discontinued to the authority which handed it over. The arrangement which gave effect to this object was virtually to constitute the prison a mortgage security for a supposed debt by the prison authority to the Government to the amount of £120 for such number of prisoners as the authority had provided with accommodation in the prison to be discontinued. Moreover, if the prison authority should have, when the prison was discontinued, received compensation in respect of having provided more accommodation than the Act required, it was required to repay such compensation to the Exchequer before receiving back the prison.

In rearranging the distribution of the prisons, power was given to the Secretary of State to set apart certain prisons for particular classes of prisoners, and it was provided that if, in pursuance of such classification, a prisoner was moved out of the jurisdiction he belonged to, he should on discharge be sent back thither at the public expense. As the closing of the prison which any authority had provided for its prisoners rendered necessary the assignment of some other prison for that purpose, the Secretary of State was empowered to substitute such other prison accordingly; and further, a general power was given to the Secretary of State to permit prisoners to be committed to a prison in an adjoining county. This provision is of obvious advantage in every way, for it enables prisoners to be sent to whichever prison is the nearest and most accessible from the place of committal, and this is in very many cases not the prison of the county.

The Prisons Act, 1877, abolished the "Visiting Justices" altogether, and transferred the powers and duties of those bodies to the Commissioners of Prisons, who now, therefore, have the sole control of the officers and the administration of the prison in regard to discipline, buildings, contracts, and expenditure of all kinds. It created, however, from among the local magistracy, a body called the Visiting Committee, whose functions are to hear and examine into reports against prisoners, and to award punishments for them; to report on any abuses within the prison which may come to their knowledge, and to hear any complaints that prisoners may make.

A curious proviso was inserted here, namely, that such complaint should be heard "in private" if asked—a proviso inserted, no doubt, on the supposition that prisoners are afraid to complain of ill-treatment, a supposition which everybody experienced in prisons knows to be belied by the number of frivolous and groundless complaints which prisoners make, and which quite ignores the consideration that, if any such complaint was kept private from the officer complained of, he could not disprove or rebut it, and that his character and position would thus be at the mercy of persons of lost character, with every motive to discredit their authority and weaken their position.

The Act diminished the punishing power of the justices by restricting their power of ordering confinement in a punishment cell to fourteen days instead of twenty-eight; and it empowered the gaoler to so confine a prisoner for only one day instead of three. The concurrence of two magistrates was made necessary to award corporal punishment. It also made an important change in the penal character of the whole sentence of imprisonment, in respect of the period for which first-class hard labour, as defined in the Prison Act, 1865, was compulsory. Under the Act of 1865 it might be enforced for any number of hours, not less than six and not more than ten daily, and for the whole of any sentence of three months, or under, it was compulsory, while it might be enforced for the entire sentence, however long. The latitude thus allowed entirely defeated the object of promoting uniformity in prison discipline, and the divergent ideas of various local authorities were further encouraged by the wide interpretation allowed by the

Home Office to the injunction which defined first-class hard labour as "tread-wheel, crank, etc. etc., or other like kind of bodily labour," for certain forms of industrial labour were allowed as "of like kind," to a labour of which the chief characteristic was that it required no skill at all, and was almost entirely penal.

It appeared on consideration that the diversity allowed in practice was rendered expedient by the strong and general feeling that the Act of 1865 went further than was necessary in allowing or encouraging this form of penal employment. The Act of 1877 therefore permitted the Secretary of State to limit the compulsory period of first-class hard labour to one month, and enabled him by the rules he was empowered to make to enforce strictly and uniformly such amount of penal labour as would be generally accepted as sufficient.

The rules of the prison in all points were henceforth to be made by the Secretary of State, so that uniformity was at least ensured on regard to diet, clothing, and discipline; and the rules were to be laid on the table of the Houses of Parliament for forty days before coming into effect. This provision may, of course, paralyse the supreme authority during six months in every year.

It is a curious fact that amidst all the improvements and ameliorations in the lot of prisoners, which previous discussion had brought about, little or no attention had been paid to the unconvicted prisoner, so that we find Sidney Smith arguing against the justice of the existing practice of requiring them to labour on the tread-wheel. The Prison Act, 1877, requires the Secretary of State to make rules for the treatment of this class of prisoner, under which a clear difference should be made between the convicted prisoner and one who is presumably innocent, and who should therefore suffer no more inconvenience than is required to ensure his safe custody, to prevent tampering with evidence, or the contrivance of plans for escape, to ensure good order and discipline necessary to be enforced in the prison, and the physical and moral wellbeing of the prisoners themselves. The Secretary of State was also empowered to make rules mitigating the treatment of persons imprisoned in default of payment ordered by a justice of the peace, and special favour was secured for the offence of sedition, by directing that any person convicted thereof should be treated as a misdemeanant of the first division, —a consideration which was also extended to persons imprisoned for contempt of court.

The prisoner who endeavours to evade the penal effect of his sentence by malingering also found his sympathising advocates in the course of the discussion on the Bill, and was protected in his schemes so far as to forbid the application of any medical test which would give him pain if he was a malingerer (but not unless) by requiring superior authority for its adoption.

In July 1877 the Royal Commissioners who were to carry this great reform into effect were appointed, and begun to prepare for the operation of the Act, which took effect from 1st April 1878. On that day, after due preparation, an order was issued by which 38 prisons of the 113 were closed in the month of May, and the reduction has been continued since then, bringing the number down to 59.

Rules were also issued constituting the visiting committees of every prison, who generally consist of about twelve members appointed by the Benches which make use of the prison, but generally assigning only one prison to each Bench for those purposes, though it might actually commit prisoners to two or more prisons.

Besides providing for the proper distribution of prisons throughout the country, and the assignment of a sufficient staff for each, with duly regulated scales of pay, the most important object of the Act was the creation of a code of rules, to embrace all matters of discipline, diet, and clothing, and to apply uniformity to all prisons. This code of rules was accordingly framed and laid for the prescribed period on the tables of the Houses of Parliament.

The duties and functions of the visiting committees are prescribed in these rules, which constitute them generally a judicial body to which a prisoner may appeal, or whose aid the governor can call in to assist him in preserving discipline, but give them no power to interfere with the administration, and carefully preserve the undivided authority of the Commissioners over the staff. They are required generally to co-operate with the Commissioners, to inspect the prison, the diets, etc., and in all matters by their presence and their influence to keep a check on the growth of abuses or neglect in the prison, informing the Commissioners of any such which may come under their cognisance.

They are empowered to permit of certain modifications of the routine of the prison in the case of a prisoner awaiting trial, or a misdemeanant of the first division, or a debtor, if they think that, having regard to his ordinary habits and condition of life, such special provision should be made in respect to him.

The prisoners awaiting trial are the subject of other rules intended to prevent them from suffering any greater disadvantage than the necessities of security and good order require, and to ensure their having every facility for conducting their defence or procuring bail.

The rules for misdemeanants of the first division guard against the possible abuse of interest or influence which might lead to an unwarrantable difference in the treatment of prisoners, by prescribing that no prisoner shall be placed in this division except as provided by statute or by order of the court of law which sentenced him. They permit the visiting committees to authorise the modification of certain ordinary rules and routine to suit the special circumstances of any particular prisoner of this class.

Special rules are also made for debtors—an offence which is popularly supposed no longer to be visited by imprisonment, and which, in fact, is so treated only by the fiction that a person who fails to pay a debt when ordered to do so by a competent court commits an act of contempt. The rules made under the Act of 1865 to suit the condition of debtors committed under the old laws, which were not repealed until 1869, are, however, held to apply to the class above referred to, who certainly are, if they are justly committed to prison at all, morally nothing less than criminals, since they refuse to pay a just debt which they have means to pay. The rules for debtors are also applied to persons imprisoned in default of finding sureties for keeping the peace or being of good behaviour, or for not complying with an order of any superior court.

The general rules for the government of prisons

provide amply for the cleanliness, good order, and humane treatment of prisoners, which form the subject of detailed instructions, which it would occupy too much space in this work to give in any fulness.

Under these rules has been introduced a system of managing the prisoners by appealing to their better qualities—described as the system of progressive stages. The principle on which this system is founded is that of setting before prisoners the advantages of good conduct and industry by enabling them to gain certain privileges or modifications of the penal character of the sentence by the exertion of these qualities. Commencing with severe penal labour—hard fare and a hard bed—he can gradually advance to more interesting employment, somewhat more material comfort, full use of library books, privilege of communication by letter and word with his friends, finally, the advantage of a moderate sum of money to start again on his discharge, so that he may not have the temptations or the excuse that want of means might afford for falling again into crime. His daily progress towards these objects is recorded by the award of marks, and any failure in industry or conduct is in the same way visited on him by forfeiture of marks and consequent postponement or diminution of the prescribed privileges.

This system, the exact opposite of governing by mere fear of punishment, must obviously have a reformatory effect; and as a means of diminishing the necessity of the more drastic forms of prison punishments, its success has been most marked, as the following returns of punishment before the prisons were transferred to Government, and since its introduction, conclusively show. The number of punishments has diminished from

61,000 to 37,000, and of the dietary punishments from 40,000 to 17,000 cases in a year.

| Year. | Daily average number of Prisoners in the year. Males & Females. | Punishment Cells. | Dietary Punishment. | Loss of Stage or Privilege. | Total Punishments. | Daily average number of Punishments per 1000 Prisoners. |
|---|---|---|---|---|---|---|
| Year ended Sept. 29, 1868 | 18,677 | 17,109 | 43,884 | .. | 60,993 | 8·9 |
| ,, ,, 1869 | 20,080 | 18,014 | 47,668 | .. | 65,682 | 8·9 |
| ,, ,, 1870 | 19,830 | 17,984 | 46,692 | .. | 64,676 | 8·9 |
| ,, ,, 1871 | 18,465 | 15,234 | 37,392 | .. | 52,626 | 7·7 |
| ,, ,, 1872 | 17,505 | 14,994 | 37,401 | .. | 52,395 | 8·1 |
| ,, ,, 1873 | 17,680 | 15,388 | 38,709 | .. | 54,097 | 8·3 |
| ,, ,, 1874 | 17,896 | 16,331 | 40,378 | .. | 56,709 | 8·6 |
| ,, ,, 1875 | 18,487 | 17,853 | 39,482 | .. | 57,335 | 8·4 |
| ,, ,, 1876 | 18,986 | 16,212 | 42,922 | .. | 59,134 | 8·5 |
| ,, ,, 1877 | 20,361 | 18,263 | 39,159 | .. | 57,422 | 7·7 |
| Six months ended March 31, 1878 | 20,833 | 9,245 | 21,986 | — | 31,231 | 8·2 |
| Year ended Mar. 31, 1879 | 19,818 | 5,164 | 36,830 | 16,908 | 58,902 | 8·1 |
| ,, ,, 1880 | 19,835 | 2,320 | 24,693 | 22,550 | 49,563 | 6·8 |
| ,, ,, 1881 | 18,027 | 2,407 | 21,846 | 18,886 | 43,139 | 6·5 |
| ,, ,, 1882 | 17,798 | 1,767 | 18,895 | 17,621 | 38,283 | 5·8 |
| ,, ,, 1883 | 17,876 | 1,869 | 19,114 | 21,400 | 42,383 | 6·4 |
| ,, ,, 1884 | 17,194 | 1,438 | 16,969 | 18,688 | 37,095 | 5·8 |

At the same time the application of the more severe punishments has been kept within strict limits by careful regulations in regard to dietary punishments, to the cases in which corporal punishment shall be inflicted, and the implements which shall be used for these purposes, to the use of punishment cells and the employment of restraint by irons or otherwise.

The moral instruction of prisoners is cared for by a chaplain of the Church of England, and when the number of Roman Catholics is sufficiently large by the appointment of a priest of their communion to attend to them. The duties of the ministers of religion require them to visit and admonish prisoners on reception and during their imprisonment; and care is taken that before discharge each prisoner shall be detained in his cell in order that full opportunity may be given for him to receive and reflect on the counsel which may be afforded him, in order to preserve him from crime in future; he then also can enter into arrangements with the Prisoners' Aid Society or otherwise for his future destination, and otherwise be fitted for discharge, and preserved from some dangers and temptations attending the change.

The literary education of the prisoner has formed the subject of very careful consideration.

Experience has shown that literary education has not the reformatory influence on prisoners which was once expected from it, and that moral and industrial instruction are the most potent of the educational influences which can be employed with that object. It is obvious that it would be bad policy to diminish the deterrent influence of penal discipline in favour of those who are ignorant; and further, that especial care ought to be taken that the education, whether literary or technical, should be carried out without sacrificing the great moral and disciplinary advantages of the separation of prisoners on which the best modern prison systems are founded. It is clear, also, that the amount of education which could be imparted to persons, who are mostly adults, in the short period for which a sentence of imprisonment endures, could in any case be but small, and although the Government might find it justifiable to incur considerably more expense than the local authorities did in providing an educational staff, it is right that a reasonable limit should be assigned to the standard of instruction which the staff should be employed to impart, and that it should devote its efforts to those who were below that standard and would most profit by such help. At the same time it is considered right that every facility and encouragement consistent with the primary object of the sentence a prisoner is undergoing should be given to those whose educational attainments might be above the standard referred to, in order that they might keep up or improve the knowledge they already possessed.

The following is an outline of the system actually adopted. It will be observed that juveniles have daily instruction in class, care being taken that juveniles awaiting trial, etc., are not brought together in class with the convicted; that the attention of the schoolmasters is confined to those adults whose education is below a certain standard, and whose sentences are long enough to make it worth while, with exceptions in the cases of those on whom, for various reasons, it would be obvious waste of labour; that those who are entirely ignorant or in that first stage of education which requires the constant personal attention of the schoolmasters, are taught in class; that those who are in a higher stage, writing copies, doing sums, learning lessons, carry on their work in their cells, and are visited by the schoolmasters, by which the evils of association and the distraction of attention are avoided.

One of the chaplains sets out the advantages of this very clearly as follows:—

Classes are, of course, held for the instruction of those who are totally ignorant of reading. In a prison of the size of our own, this is, I fear, unavoidable, though, from a disciplinary point of view, certainly to be deprecated. It is scarcely possible to entirely prevent all communication, and this communication means the spread of corrupting influences. I do my best to make these classes as small as possible.

Considering that prisoners should look upon education as a privilege, and convinced of the great advantage of preserving the specially penal character of the first month of the sentence, on account of the deterring effect on the criminal, and because it is the foundation of the progressive stage system, by which such a large diminution of prison punishment has been effected, prisoners are not allowed the relaxation which the class or the visits of the schoolmasters afford until they have, by their industry and good conduct, gained promotion to the second stage, which they can do in one month.

Prisoners are stimulated to endeavour to improve themselves by a regulation that those who desire at the periodical time to exercise their privilege of writing to their friends shall do it with their own hands after a certain period of instruction.

The chaplains are required to examine prisoners periodically to test their progress.

The teaching staff, which was entirely absent in a great many prisons under the local authorities, has been increased and distributed according to a definite plan, and now costs £2230 per annum more than under the local authorities, although the prison population is some 20 per cent less.

### Summary of Regulations on Education in Prisons.

All juveniles under sixteen have one hour's instruction daily in class, excepting, of course, any who by statute or rule are not allowed to be mixed with others.

All prisoners, except juveniles, whose sentences do not fall below four months, are on reception examined by the chaplain and divided into classes as under:—

Class I. Those who cannot read Standard I. of the National Society's reading-book.

Class II. Those who can read Standard I., but have not reached Standard III.

Class III. Those who have reached Standard III.

Prisoners in Classes I. and II., whose age does not exceed forty years, receive instruction in reading, writing, and arithmetic, subject to conditions. In special cases prisoners above that age may receive instruction.

Prisoners found to have no capacity for learning, or who are idle, are excluded from instruction, the latter, however, only temporarily; and prisoners previously convicted may, if found advisable, be excluded.

Prisoners in Class III. receive instruction only in writing and arithmetic, if they need it, but they are furnished with books, together with slate and pencil, to enable them to improve themselves.

The limits of instruction are:—

*Reading*, as far as Standard III. inclusive.

*Writing*, as far as transcribing a portion of the book read, and reading what has been transcribed.

*Arithmetic*, as far as casting simple money accounts, and mental calculation of small money sums.

Prisoners in Class I. are taught reading collectively in a room or place provided for the purpose. All other teaching is conducted separately in the cells.

When a prisoner can read Standard II. with fluency he is allowed a library book in his cell.

The lessons given to prisoners in their cells are not

less than two lessons weekly, of a quarter of an hour each if possible, with an interval of two days at least.

The collective instruction consist of two lessons weekly, of half an hour each (exclusive of the time occupied in assembling and removing the prisoners), with a like interval.

All prisoners receiving instruction are tested by actual examination by the chaplain or assistant chaplain on admission, and prior to their discharge, the results of each examination being recorded by the chaplain in his educational register.

In order to stimulate prisoners to take advantage of these opportunities, those who are in the second and third class, who are by the rules entitled to write a letter, are required to do so for themselves, and not to have letters written for them except in special cases; and prisoners in the first class on reception may have not more than two letters written for them except in special cases.

A uniform diet has been established for all prisons, framed with due respect to both scientific principles and practical knowledge.

There is perhaps hardly any subject of prison treatment on which more discussion has taken place and more theories been broached than that of diets. The House of Lords' Committee of 1862 commented on "the total absence of uniformity and the irreconcilable inequalities in the nature and amount of the food given." At that time there was a dietary recommended by the Home Office in 1843, but only 63 out of 140 local prisons adhered to it, and the dietary framed in 1864, in hopes of promoting greater uniformity, were even still less successful, for many continued to adhere to the old scale, and the new was adopted only by 26 prisons out of 114. The following instructions were issued to a committee of medical gentlemen practically conversant with prison administration, who were appointed to frame a diet for general adoption:—

MEMORANDUM of Instructions to the Committee appointed to consider and Report upon the Dietaries of Local Prisons.

They are requested to consider and report on the subject of diets for prisoners in local gaols, with a view to introducing uniformity as far as possible throughout the various prisons in England and Wales.

They are requested also to frame diets suitable for the various classes of prisoners specified in the Prisons Acts, 1865 and 1877, distinguishing between male and female prisoners, adults and children, and those sentenced with or without hard labour.

For this purpose they are requested to examine, so far as may be necessary for this inquiry, any diets now in use in the local gaols, and to satisfy themselves by whatever inquiry they think necessary from all available sources of their respective effects upon the health of the prisoners, as well as their relation to discipline, to capacity for work, and to crime. In carrying out this investigation the Committee are requested to bear in mind the want of uniformity that has hitherto existed with regard to labour and discipline.

To consider whether it is desirable to frame different diets for different districts, or whether the same scale will serve for all districts.

To consider whether it is expedient that prisoners sentenced to short periods of imprisonment should be placed on a different diet from that of persons sentenced to longer periods. In the event of the adoption of the principle of variation of diet with length of sentences, the Committee are requested to report whether, in their opinion, prisoners under long sentences should be placed at once upon the dietary belonging to such sentences, or should pass through these successive dietaries belonging to the shorter sentences.

With respect to employment, the Committee are instructed that the provisions of the Prisons Act of 1865, by which first-class hard labour is imposed on all adult male prisoners during the first three months of their sentences, can be, and probably will be, altered under the Act of 1877, by limiting that class of labour to one month, and they are requested to consider whether the diets should vary according as the employment is hard or light. In framing or recommending the dietaries for the several classes of male and female prisoners, the Committee are requested to avoid any approach either to indulgence or to excess, but to arrange that the diet shall be sufficient and not more than sufficient to maintain health and strength; and to consider whether any rules can be laid down for establishing adequate checks upon the practice of ordering extra diets, or for the guidance of medical officers on this point.

The Committee are desired to ascertain whether any one of the diets now in use is likely to fulfil the requirements which may be deemed necessary, and whether, if such a diet be found, it would be expedient to recommend it for general adoption in preference to framing a new scale.

The Committee are requested to compare the cost of the dietaries, which they may deem it their duty to recommend, with the actual cost of the dietaries now in use (see Judicial Statistics and Reports of the Inspectors of Prisons).

The Committee are requested to prepare or recommend scales of hospital diet for male and female adults, and for boys and girls.

Also to consider whether, and how far, a reduction in diet can be made to secure the purposes of punishment for prison offences, and under what system.

In conducting their deliberations on the important subject referred to them, the Committee are requested to keep constantly in view the various influences to which prisoners are exposed, some of which, such as climate and changes of season, are common to all; while others, such as loss of liberty and the restraints of discipline, are peculiar to the state of imprisonment.

They are requested, moreover, in preparing their report, to take into careful consideration the various collateral subjects, such as clothing, temperature, hours of labour, sleep, and exercise, which are especially and intimately related to food supply, and which consequently exercise an important practical bearing upon the working of prison scales of diet.

In order to solve the questions put before them, the Committee were under the necessity of inquiring into the truth of various theories which had found more or less acceptance, one in particular, under which it was considered that the depression of mind resulting from imprisonment should be and could be prevented from having an injurious bodily effect by increasing the diet, a theory which, they pointed out, omitted to take into consideration that, "in a large number of cases," imprisonment, as now conducted, is a condition more or less akin to that of "physiological rest,"—"of freedom of much worry and anxiety,"—of abundance of rest, with ample warmth and clothing: compensating effects on the bodily condition, even if depression of mind could properly be counteracted by taking in more food. As regards the question of principle raised in the several paragraphs of the instructions above quoted, they say:—

"1. The first question, as to the expediency of variation of diet with length of sentence, admits, we think, of a ready reply. It appears to us to be a self-evident proposition that imprisonment should be rendered as deterrent as is consistent with the maintenance of health and strength, whatever may be the sentence, and we think that the shorter the term of imprisonment the more strongly should the penal element be manifested in the diet. It is a matter of universal experience that partial abstinence from food for a limited period is not only safe under ordinary circumstances, but frequently beneficial, and we think that a spare diet is all that is necessary for a prisoner undergoing a sentence of a few days or weeks. To give such a prisoner a diet necessary for the maintenance of health during the longer terms would, in our opinion, be to forego an opportunity for the infliction of salutary punishment; it would constitute an encouragement to the commission of petty crimes; and, by thus paving the way to indulgence in the more serious class of offences, would assist in the manufacture of the habitual criminal.

"Without dwelling further upon this subject, we may at once say that we accept the principle of variation of diet with length of sentence as being theoretically sound and practically desirable.

"2. The question as to whether prisoners under long sentences should be placed at once upon the dietary proper to their class, or should be made to pass through the successive dietaries belonging to the shorter sentences, received the careful attention of the Committee of 1864, and, on referring to the report of that Committee, we find that they embrace the principle 'which commends itself to their judgment as most consistent with common sense and common justice, namely, that all prisoners, without exception, shall graduate through the dietaries proper to all the sentences shorter than their own until they reach the dietary proper to their own class.' They consider that the ends of justice are in a serious measure defeated by at once giving the more guilty criminal a diet which is in striking contrast with that received by a prisoner who has committed some comparatively trifling offence, and they recommend that *all* prisoners shall commence with the *lowest* diet, unless specially exempted by the medical officer.

"The Committee appointed in 1867 to inquire into the dietaries of the county and burgh gaols of Ireland entertain a very different view, and express themselves as follows :—

"What has been termed a 'progressive dietary,' in other words, the placing prisoners sentenced to hard labour during the early periods of their incarceration on the lowest scale of food, has been carefully considered.

"We have no hesitation in saying that such a procedure must be attended with the worst results.

"It is at the first period of imprisonment that want of liberty is most keenly felt by the prisoner; there may be remorse for the crime committed which led to imprisonment, or chagrin at the detection of that crime, a craving for the too frequent stimulants; in short, everything combines to depress the vital powers; then, if in addition to these, the allowance of food be barely sufficient to sustain life, how can the hard-labour sentence be carried out? The prisoner cannot do the work, health fails, the surgeon is called for, and extra diet is the inevitable result.

"Notwithstanding, however, that the first Committee embrace the principle of progressive diets as being 'most consistent with common sense,' and that the second stigmatise it as a 'procedure which must be attended with the worst results,' we find, on further perusal of the reports of the two Committees, that the difference between them is not so great as might be gathered from the contradictory character of the opinions just quoted.

"We have no hesitation in saying that there is some truth in both creeds, and that a middle course between the two is that which will be found most likely to ensure safety and to be conducive to the attainment of the objects in view.

"The objections usually raised to progressive dietaries are relevant only to cases in which that principle is carried to its fullest extent; they refer, in fact, only to a particular system by which the principle is applied, and not to the principle itself. The advantages of the progressive principle may be retained without incurring any risk of inflicting injury; and we shall presently point out the means by which this may be effected."

They say, "The question as to what is 'sufficiency' in a prison scale of diet, though often discussed, is probably destined never to receive a conclusive and generally convincing answer; for sufficiency is not a quantity capable of demonstration. There is, at the outset, the defect inherent in all scales, that a uniform diet is given to persons of various age, weight, height, idiosyncrasy, and physical conformation; but scales will nevertheless be always rendered necessary by the exigencies of administration, not only in prisons, but in fleets and armies, and wherever bodies of persons must be dealt with in the mass. It is the duty of those who are called upon to frame scales of diet to be guided by averages, and it is the duty of those who use them to provide for exceptional cases by special means. The question of sufficiency cannot be dealt with entirely apart from that of cost; and we conceive that we should ill discharge our functions if we were to lose sight of the fact that prisoners are, to some extent, maintained at the expense of those whom they have injured. We feel that we have a duty to the public which cannot be ignored; and that it should be our object to meet the just requirements of the prisoners without setting up attractions which would be likely to increase the number of committals."

They say, "The question raised in the fifth paragraph of our instructions, as to 'whether it is desirable to frame different diets for different districts, or whether the same diet will serve for all districts, has received our very careful consideration, and we have deemed it our duty to collect opinions and information on this subject from various sources. We find that the differences in the diet of free labourers in different parts of the country relate less to nutritive value than to the form in which the nutriment is taken, and that the variations in quantity and relative proportions of nutritive elements and proximate constituents, are not considerable in cases in which the amount of work performed is fairly comparable. The diet of the various classes of mechanics and artisans appears to be but little influenced by locality, and in the ranks above them all such differences vanish. We have failed to discover any such contrasts between different districts as to warrant us in transgressing upon that uniformity which our instructions inform us is one of the chief objects to be kept in view. If we were to take existing prison dietaries as our guide, we should in some cases find it necessary to make greater differences between two neighbouring counties than between districts hundreds of miles apart. And if we were to be guided by general impressions as to the manifold requirements of persons who have followed different occupations previous to imprisonment, we should bring about 'irreconcilable inequalities' even more serious than those of which the Select Committee of the House of Lords so much complained. We are told that the operatives of Lancashire have larger appetites than agricultural labourers, and we reply that appetite is no criterion as to what is necessary. We are told that miners consume large quantities of meat, and we reply that they also consume large quantities of beer and tobacco, but that we should not for that reason be justified in introducing such luxuries into our dietary. Ironworkers are said to be accustomed to 'rich' food; on the other hand, the Irish labourer, in Liverpool, looks to bulk, and his ideal dinner is half a stone of potatoes. We should find it extremely difficult to gratify these different tastes, and think that no good object would be attained by any attempt to do so. Hitherto, it has been left to the discretion of the local authorities to act upon the recommendations of the Home Office, or to frame and adopt dietaries of their own, subject, of course, to the sanction of the Secretary of State, and it is worthy of remark that the allowance of meat is, in many cases, less liberal to prisoners in the mining and manufacturing districts than to those drawn from rural populations. We have pointed out at page 18 that the Class V. diet of 1843, which is comparatively rich in animal food, serves as the basis of the diet of the longer terms in a considerable number of prisons; but that it is adopted without alteration, less in mining and manufacturing districts than in those in which agriculture is the leading occupation. Taking into careful consideration all the information that we have obtained on this subject, we are of opinion that there is nothing in the habits of the classes from which prisoners are chiefly drawn to render it necessary that the diet of any one or more districts within the limits of England and Wales should differ from that of the rest."

As regards *extra diet* they say, "We find, on perusal of our instructions, that indulgence and excess are referred to as practices which should be restricted, and we are desired to consider whether any rules can be laid down by which adequate checks upon such practices can be established.

"We are of opinion that, in some prisons, the dietary scales now in use are, in certain respects, in excess of actual requirements; and we would point out that an abatement of this excess would naturally follow from the adoption of a dietary which would be *de facto* 'sufficient and not more than sufficient' to maintain health and strength. We find, however, that independently of the particular scale of diet adopted, there is an excess which takes the form of 'extra' diet, this extra diet consisting occasionally of articles sent out from the hospital, but more generally of an additional allowance of bread, or of the substitution of the diet of one class for that of another. It might, *a priori*, be expected that the issue of extras would bear some relation to the comparative sufficiency or insufficiency of the regular scale of diet, and so it does, but the relation is the reverse of that which might reasonably have been thought probable. As a general rule, we find that extra diet is given most freely, not in those prisons in which the ordinary scale is relatively scanty, but in those in which it fully reaches the average, or is even above it, and we think that this may, in some cases at least, be explained by the fact that the same considerations which have influenced the Governing Committee in the adoption of a comparatively liberal scale have also tended to encourage the executive authorities in liberally setting it at nought. We have no reason to believe that the health of the prisoners in establishments in which extras are given with a free hand reaches a higher standard than is attained in prisons in which the extras are issued with discrimination, and are limited to strictly exceptional cases. In more than one prison it is the rule to issue extra bread to any prisoner who has lost a few pounds in weight, on the assumption that loss of weight is sufficient proof of impairment of health. We agree with the Committee of 1864 that this assumption must be viewed with suspicion, as resting upon an insecure foundation. The same Committee draw attention to a second assumption, namely, 'that the weight of the body is not greatly affected, in short periods of time, by other than dietetic causes,' and we agree with them that this supposition also can easily be proved to be unsound, and 'that fluctuations in weight bearing no sort of proportion to the increase, decrease, or change of diet by which they were preceded are of constant occurrence.'

"The test of weight has a certain value when made use of as one among other tests of sufficiency or insufficiency of diet; but to trust to it alone, and to lose sight of the fact that fluctuations in weight are due, not to one, but to many causes, is unreasonable, and must lead to unnecessary interference with discipline.

"But although we think that much of the extra food now given is unnecessary, we do not recommend the adoption of any rules which would fetter the action of officers who are responsible for the health and wellbeing of the prisoners under their charge. The medical officer should, in our judgment, continue in possession of the power of recommending the issue of extra diet to any prisoner whose bodily condition or state of health is such as to render it necessary to make some addition to the ordinary diet of his class. We have only to suggest that the grounds on which the increase is made be entered in a journal provided for the purpose, and that in cases in which it is necessary to continue the additional diet for a period exceeding one month, the recommendation be renewed, an entry at the same time being made showing the reason for such renewal. The responsibilities of the medical officer would thus remain unaffected, his powers in relation to those who are really in need of his good offices would be increased rather than diminished, and he would from time to time be reminded that any departure from the established scale is in itself undesirable, and should not be recommended without good and sufficient reason."

It is not desirable to encumber this work with details of the actual diet adopted, which can easily be ascertained by those to whom it is of interest, but it may suffice to say that there is now one diet for the prisons of the whole of England and Wales, that it is believed to be a better diet than the generality of those formerly in use, and that from this and other causes the health of the prisons is certainly higher; but that from careful study of the ingredients, the cost of food for prisoners is now less than it used to be.

The staff of the prisons are, of course, all appointed by the Government, and the formation of all the prisons into one department has had the great advantage of opening out to all the opportunity of promotion offered by the wider area. The antecedents of all candidates are carefully inquired into, the most promising are selected, and these are required further to pass the ordeal of Civil Service examination and inquiry into character. The following admirable order, originally issued by Lord Palmerston, for application to the convict prisons, has been extended to the local prisons :—

Whereas it has happened in several instances that officers in the convict service have attempted to obtain their promotion by means of applications from private friends, and whereas such practices are injurious to the good order and discipline of the service, notice is hereby given that all officers of the convict service must understand that their prospects of promotion must depend on the report their superiors may make as to their qualifications, and as to their conduct in the performance of their duties. Merit and not favour will thus be the ground of advancement, and any officer who may attempt to bring private interest to bear for the purpose of influencing the Directors to promote him will be considered as having disqualified himself for the promotion which he may thus have sought to obtain.

In sanitary matters, especially in regard to construction, prisons were certainly a great deal in advance of other establishments, public or private, and the construction of the prison at Pentonville in 1840, as a model for all others, has resulted in a high standard being maintained throughout this country. But the natural consequence of the local prisons being under so many independent authorities, of whom many did not appreciate the full importance of the subject, and few were likely to possess knowledge on it up to the highest level attained, was that they did not keep abreast of advancing experience. It became the duty, therefore, of the newly-formed Prison Department to remedy all these deficiencies, and to complete the replacing of the old style of prisons by those of most modern design, where the local authorities had failed to do so.

A large proportion of the prisoners who form the population of our prisons are of diseased and impaired constitutions, victims of dirt, intemperance, and irregularity, and the sins of the fathers in these respects are visited on the children "to the third and fourth generation." The accurate medical examination of these on reception, the cleansing of them and their clothing from vermin and dirt, the due apportionment of labour, and, in many cases, their immediate medical treatment, have necessitated the provision of proper reception buildings, apart from the rest of the prison, where these processes can be carried on, and risk of carrying infection into the prison obviated. The hospital accommodation has had to be improved, and separate wards for contagious diseases provided, and generally the medical service of the prison much improved.

A Committee was appointed shortly after the commencement of the Act to decide what form of penal or first-class hard labour should be adopted for general use, and the result was that the tread-wheel has been generally introduced. The task of tread-wheel work has been also made uniform, and now instead of a prisoner having in one prison to ascend 7200 feet in a day, and 12,852 in another, all have to perform the uniform task of 8640 feet, at the rate of 32 feet ascent per minute during a period of six hours, divided into two equal portions, in which they work by spells of fifteen minutes' labour and five minutes' resting.

The Commissioners soon observed the necessity for providing quarters for the warders, etc., in proximity to the prison, and especially the necessity of doing so in towns where the rents are high, and the officers likely to be thrown into undesirable contact with a certain class of the population in their search for lodgings within their means. Considerable progress has already been made in this direction.

A general inquiry into the security of the prisons has led to the removal of many defects which carelessness or inexperience had allowed to grow up.

In the designing and execution of all these building works an undeniable economy, both of power and money, has attended the transfer of this duty to the Government; for instead of each local authority employing its own architect (paid by commission on the expenditure), whose plans had to be approved by the Surveyor-General before they could be carried out (a process involving trouble and correspondence, and not always ensuring good results), the responsibility is thrown direct on the Surveyor-General himself; and instead of contractors and paid labour being universally employed, very considerable use is made of the prisoners' labour in the buildings and repairs, so that it is estimated that the expenditure in buildings has produced results which would have cost £50,000 per annum more than they actually have under the present system. In this department also the concentration of experience and responsibility has had and must continue to have the result of bringing all prisons in this most important matter up to the standard of the highest; but in one respect the Government is at present at a great disadvantage. If a local authority determined to rebuild its prison, or execute any important work connected with it, they could, with Treasury sanction, borrow the money and do the work at once, and spread the repayment over thirty years. This system is not permissible for the Government without a special Act of Parliament, and if many of the local authorities had not during many years continuously made great efforts to furnish themselves with the best type of prison buildings, but had left it for Government to do, it may be doubted whether the country would in any reasonable time have been in so good a position as it actually is in regard to prison buildings.

The objects which the Prisons Act, 1877, was intended to secure were two, viz. the application to all prisoners, wherever confined, of a uniform system of punishment, devised to effect in the best method that which is the great object of punishment, viz. the repression of crime; and economy in the expenses of prisons. It may not have been intended to place the administration of prisons under authority more effectively responsible to public opinion than the numerous bodies of local justices could be; but it has no doubt had this further effect, for every occurrence in a prison may now become a subject of discussion in Parliament.

It is difficult, indeed impossible, to make such comparisons of the statistics of prisons before and after 1878 as should eliminate all causes but those which have flowed from the Act of 1877, and so to show the results of that Act. Some measures have come into force of late years which would tend to increase the prison population, such as the penal clauses of the Education Act, of various Local Acts empowering the enforcement of by-laws by imprisonment, and of the Licensing Acts and the Prevention of Crime Acts; others to decrease it, as the Summary Jurisdiction Acts, 1879, which gave power to inflict fines for some offences instead of imprisonment, and allowed magistrates to give time for payment of a fine, and made it in some cases a civil debt, in others reducing the scale of imprisonment in default. The closing of several military prisons in 1869, and the committal of some of the soldiers sentenced by court-martial to local prisons, increased the population of the latter somewhat, and the re-establishment of military prisons in 1880-81 diminished it similarly; but these reservations are only necessary so far as to indicate that the figures which mark the great improvement which has taken place of late years must be considered as illustrating, but not precisely measuring, the results of the Act.

The following is a brief comparative summary of various important features in regard to the condition of the local prisons before the Prison Act, 1877, came into operation, and at the present time:—

1. The number of prisons has been reduced from 113 to 59, while the gross amount of prison accommodation is only reduced from 27,392 to about 23,089.

2. The number of the staff has been largely diminished, and the cost of the staff, and of the maintenance of the prisons, has been reduced.

This diminution in the staff and its cost is the more noteworthy, because the cost of staff under the local authorities rose continuously from 1857, when it was £179,791, to £239,247 in 1878, when it was handed over to the Government; and these amounts did not include all the emoluments (valued at several thousands) of the officers concerned.

STATEMENT showing the reduction in the number of Superior Officers of Local Prisons and of the gross value of their Salaries and Emoluments.

| | | Governors. | Chaplains. | Medical Officers. | Matrons. | Total. | Reduction. |
|---|---|---|---|---|---|---|---|
| On taking over the local prisons in April 1878. | Number . . | 111 | 113 | 112 | 110 | 446 | 213 |
| | Salaries and emoluments | £49,110 | £22,895 | £13,605 | £10,183 | £95,793 | £ 95,793 |
| When new arrangements are completely carried into effect. | Number . . | 59 | 59 | 59 | 56 | 233 | 54,922 |
| | Salaries and emoluments | £22,673 | £15,286 | £11,596 | £5,347 | £54,922 | 40,871 |

There is, therefore, a saving of £40,871 per annum in the salaries of superior officers, of which nearly all has been already realised. It must be noted that this has been effected concurrently with an increase in the expenses due to the improvement of the position of the medical staff. An increase of charge due to the general payment of Roman Catholic priests, amounting to £1207, is not taken into account in these figures.

The subordinate staff has also been diminished somewhat by the concentration of prisons, but has been increased by the addition of a school staff throughout, and by additions to the clerical staff, prisoners not being allowed now in the offices, so that on this point the change has had its result in improved administration rather than in any marked financial saving.

A considerable reduction in the charge for ordinary

repairs has, of course, followed on the reduction in the number of prisons. That item from 1857 to 1877 averaged £21,500 per annum. Since then it has averaged £11,425 per annum. It is, of course, possible that, under the local authorities, some expenditure may have been charged to this item which should not strictly have been so classified; and, on the other hand, it is known that items of considerable magnitude did not pass through the prison books, and so were not recorded in the returns from which the cost of prisons in former years is ascertained.

It will easily be understood that the reduction in the number of prisons must have resulted in a saving in fuel and light, but the total cost of these items is so much influenced by the market prices of the year and the character of the season that it is impossible to say how much effect the closing of prisons alone has had; but some instances of the result of careful supervision may illustrate the effect of this consequence of the Prison Act.

The consumption of gas in seven prisons has, by care, been reduced from 15,009,710 feet to 12,673,400 feet in a year. This would amount for these few prisons to nearly £300 per annum.

The consumption of coal and coke in six prisons has been reduced in like manner from 5833 tons to 5238 tons. This would amount to about £240 a year.

At one large prison, by concentrating the cooking and baking arrangements, and also by reorganising the steam boilers and engines and by other improvements of that nature, a saving of £886 per annum in fuel and staff has been effected.

As one of the instances of the saving which has resulted from the system of administration introduced after the Prison Act, may be mentioned an economy in conveyance of prisoners sentenced to penal servitude. Under the local authorities each prison sent its prisoners to the convict prisons without any reference to what other prisons might be doing, and consequently single prisoners, accompanied by two warders, constantly came up from distant prisons, although some adjoining prisons had men to send up who might conveniently have been taken charge of by the same escort. The Commissioners have adopted a plan of collecting the prisoners of each locality in certain centres and sending them all together periodically. It is anticipated that there will be a saving of some hundreds of pounds a year in travelling by this arrangement, which could not have been adopted except under present conditions. A saving in hiring officers to replace those on escort will also follow.

In the matter of cost a comparison between one year and another is so much affected by fluctuating conditions, such as the price of provisions, etc., and the number of prisoners, that such comparisons require a great deal of correction; moreover the accounts of cost before 1878 are most imperfect and unsystematic. Making, however, the best of our material, and taking the aggregate or the average of a number of years, it is found that the gross total expenditure from 1st April 1878 till 31st March 1885, and of a corresponding number of years preceding 1877, exclusive in both cases of certain items which do not properly enter into the comparison, is as follows:—

| | | | | | | | | |
|---|---|---|---|---|---|---|---|---|
| | 1870-71 | 1871-72 | 1872-73 | 1873-74 | 1874-75 | 1875-76 | 1876-77 | Total of 7 years. |
| Under local authority . | £ 456,760 | £ 452,100 | £ 479,990 | £ 484,659 | £ 474,719 | £ 485,479 | £ 496,870 | £ 3,330,577 |
| | 1878-79 | 1879-80 | 1880-81 | 1881-82 | 1882-83 | 1883-84 | 1884-85 | |
| Under government . . . | £ 396,352 | £ 450,956 | £ 437,074 | £ 386,113 | £ 400,729 | £ 389,791 | £ 381,400 | £ 2,842,455 |

There has been already, therefore. an economy amounting to hard upon half a million of money, in spite of certain increases of expenditure for the improvement of the service. Moreover a large number of valuable sites occupied by unnecessary prisons have been set free for more useful purposes.

3. The religious needs of the Roman Catholic prisoners have been more generally provided for by the more extended employment of paid Roman Catholic priests.
4. A uniform treatment and discipline has been applied to all prisons founded on the most approved experience.
5. A uniform and improved dietary has been introduced into all prisons, and the means of cooking have been much improved where necessary; while the diet is better, though less costly, and improved supervision tends to prevent waste.
6. Sanitary requirements have received considerable attention; and less money, by a considerable amount, is spent in medicine.

All prisoners are, of course, completely cleansed in their persons and so far as possible, the clothes of all are washed before their discharge, besides being disinfected and freed from vermin. A somewhat remarkable illustration of the domestic condition of the criminal population, tending to show a close connection between a low moral and a low social condition, is afforded by a report of the "sanitary danger arising from the exceedingly dirty condition of a large number of prisoners on their reception, both as respects their bodies and their clothes." The governor of Clerkenwell prison reported that he found extreme difficulty, notwithstanding the most strenuous care and precaution, in guarding against vermin; that prisoners are received covered with lice, so that they drop off going down the passage; and that he had been told by a prisoner that he had broken a window in order to get into prison to be cleansed of his vermin.

7. The yearly average death-rate for the five and a half years ended 31st March 1878 was 10·8 per 1000, while for the six years ended 31st March 1885 it was 8·2 per 1000.
8. The yearly average number of suicides in the five and a half years ended 31st March 1878 was 17·6, while in the six years ended 31st March 1885 it was 13·8.
9. The yearly average number of cases in which corporal punishment was inflicted in the five and a half years ended 31st March 1878 was 11·13 per 1000, while for the six years ended 31st March 1885 it was 9·8 per 1000.
10. The yearly average number of cases in which dietary punishment was inflicted in the five and a half years ended 31st March 1878 was 40,770, while for the six years ended 31st March 1885 it was 19,820, and much fewer in late years,

since the system of progressive stages has been more fully taken advantage of. This diminution in the number of cases of this class of punishment has been effected notwithstanding that the severity of these punishments has been diminished both by the Act and by orders.

11. A greater variety of employment has been introduced, many new industries being now followed in substitution of that of mat-making, and supplies for prison use and buildings formerly furnished by free labour and contract are now made by prison labour.

12. The accounts have been established on a clear and uniform system, the necessary stocktakings and other proper checks against misappropriation have been introduced. The employment of prisoners as clerks—a most undesirable feature of the former management, adopted no doubt from motives of economy,—has been put an end to.

13. The amount of money granted for aid to prisoners on discharge has been increased from a yearly average of £3801 to £7280. The grants to prisoners through the direct agency of the Aid Societies is fixed, provided that certain conditions are fulfilled, at £4000, as compared with a yearly average of £1791, which was formerly given by local authorities through those institutions.

The concentration of administration of all prisons has made it possible to collect certain statistics showing the general flow and disposal of the prison population to be as under from an average of six years :—

| | |
|---|---|
| The average number at the beginning of the year has been . . . . . . . | 18,033 |
| Number received yearly . . . . | 193,485 |
| Number removed to convict and other local prisons, schools, and reformatories . . | 8,125 |
| Discharged on pardon or commutation, license, termination of sentence, or commitment and bailed after committal . . . | 185,504 |
| Removed to lunatic asylum . . . . | 164 |
| Escaped . . . . . . . . | 5 |
| Died from natural causes . . . . | 152 |
| Committed suicide . . . . . . | 14 |
| Executed . . . . . . . . | 12 |

They also show the fluctuation of crime in different months and different years, which may be of use in tracing the causes of crime, indicating the means of diminishing it, and testing the success of those which may be adopted. They certainly dispel certain incorrect ideas on the subject, for it has been very commonly alleged that crime prevails in the winter months, when employment is less plentiful and the comfort afforded by a prison acceptable, than in the summer. This is shown to be as far from the truth as it is possible to be, for taking the prison population as the measure of the prevalence of crime, it is found from combining into an average the observation of seven years, that while the prison population is about the same in June and December, it is always above that number from June to December, and always below it from December to June; it rises to its highest point about October and falls to its lowest about February; the highest population of the year is about 600 above the

June and December level, and the lowest is 1000 below it, making a total difference between October and February of 1600 prisoners, or about 10 per cent.

The fluctuations in the average population of prisoners, during a term of years, measured in the same way, are very remarkable. I have been able to obtain accurate statistics from 1851, and have compared the average fluctuations of pauper population with that of the prisons. There does not appear to be any correspondence between the two if the outdoor and indoor pauper population combined are considered, but a remarkable coincidence for a term of years, and an equally remarkable divergence afterwards is revealed if the indoor pauper population are compared with the prison population. Both fell from 1851 to 1853, and both then commenced to rise. The pauper population attained its summit, and commenced falling in 1856, the criminal did the same in 1857; both fell till 1860, and then commenced rising; both rose till 1863, and then commenced falling; both then fell till 1866, and then commenced rising. The criminal population rose till 1869, the pauper population rose till 1870, after these dates both fell. In 1872 commenced a complete divergence after twenty years of complete correspondence, for at that date the pauper population continued its downward course till 1876, while crime continued to rise till 1877, and at these two dates the pauper population began to rise and the prison population to fall. The rise in the pauper population continued till 1883, as did the fall of the prison population, and only after the latter year did the direction of the fluctuation again correspond, for in that year both the pauper and the criminal population fell.

During the part of the present year, 1885, which has yet passed, the prison population has touched and continued at a lower level than we have ever known it; and, in fact, whereas the prison population was, the day after the prisons were transferred to Government on 2d April 1878, 20,442, and in June 1878 the highest known, so far as can be ascertained, viz. 21,030, it has since almost continuously fallen until, in February 1885, it has touched the lowest figure known, viz. 15,484, and on 2d June 1885 it was 15,733; and there is this satisfactory feature about the present condition of affairs, that the prison population has for several years successively continued at a low level, which it never has done before. In fact statistics show that generally the prison population has alternately risen and fallen during periods of three years; and we should therefore have expected that the fall which commenced in 1878 would have continued till 1881, and then been followed by a rise till 1884, but in fact the numbers have either continued low or fallen lower during all the seven years following 1877.

It certainly seems justifiable to infer from these figures that our penal reformatory system has been made effective; and the remarkably steady and sustained decrease in our prison population of late years must be considered to show that recent legislation with which it so remarkably coincides in point of time has in principle and in execution not only completely succeeded in its object of promoting uniformity, economy, and improved administration, but also in that which is the main purpose of all, the repression of crime.

# CHAPTER V.

## TRANSPORTATION.

THAT particular form of imprisonment with hard labour which is termed "penal servitude" has a different history to that of ordinary imprisonment, and the present system cannot be understood and appreciated without a knowledge of the transportation system from which it is derived. The following sketch of its development is taken mainly from an article furnished by me to the *Nineteenth Century*, and here republished by permission.

It was not established to accord with any *à priori* reasoning, nor to suit abstract theoretical principles, but has grown up, like most other English institutions, by successive alterations and improvements which have been made in accordance with the varying circumstances of the country and the demands of public feeling, and may be considered the result of the thought and deliberation of some of our greatest statesmen, guided and assisted by the experience of those whose practical connection with the subject has enabled them to study it in the way in which alone reliable information can be gained and sound opinions can be formed.

The Parliamentary reports and correspondence published by Government during the period of transportation give a vast deal of information as to the working of our system of secondary punishments throughout that period, especially that of the Select Committee of 1838. This was a remarkable epoch in the history of the system, as it was then that it had received its greatest development, so far as respects the number of persons subjected to it—the number of offenders who were sent out of the country in 1834 having been 4920, falling gradually to 3805 in 1838. The total number of convicts sent to Australia during the continuance of the system was 134,308.

The foundation, or earliest phase, of the punishment appears to have been simply exile or banishment, which required only departure from the realm, but without assigning any particular locality, and attended with no compulsory labour. Compulsory banishment is expressly forbidden by Magna Charta; but, when it was offered as an alternative against something worse, of course many offenders were glad to accept it, as it were voluntarily. To the felon who had taken sanctuary the choice of self-banishment was offered with the condition that the hanging he had escaped would be inflicted if he did not depart speedily, or in case he should ever return. The right of sanctuary afterwards came to include the privilege of living within the precincts of the place of sanctuary, free from molestation, to a specified number of persons, but was put an end to by statute in the reign of James I. (though for another century it existed as against civil process in defiance of law), and consequently the system of self-banishment, as founded on it; but before that time, exile or banishment, as it was termed, had been legally established.

In the reign of Henry VIII. crime appears to have increased to such an alarming extent as to call for special and severe measures of repression. It is said to have been due to the pauperism which followed the abolition of the monasteries; but as the monasteries merely changed hands, falling into possession of laymen or others, who no doubt continued whatever useful remunerative work the monasteries had carried on, it is not easy to see how the measure can have created such poverty, unless it was that the funds of the monasteries maintained troops of idlers, who, when their means of subsistence without working were withdrawn, resolved themselves into "great thieves, petty rogues, and vagabonds." But, whatever may have been the cause, there is no doubt of the existence of a very great deal of crime, or of the severe measures taken to repress it.

In the reign of Queen Elizabeth other means were resorted to. The passing of poor laws was designed to remove the temptation to crime presented by extreme and hopeless poverty, and the fulness of the prisons was relieved by banishing those who were subject to such punishment. According to the best authorities, banishment was introduced as a punishment by the Legislature in the thirty-ninth year of Elizabeth, the expense of the banishment to be paid by the counties and boroughs. The same Act encouraged the establishment of houses of correction by justices and private persons, on the model of the Bridewell Hospital, a palace near Blackfriars, given by Edward VI. to the City of London, and endowed by him as a lodging-house for the tramps of those days, and for the correction of vagabonds, harlots, and idle persons, and for finding them work.

"Transportation" was introduced in the reign of Charles II., and might be inflicted (1) by the justices at their quarter sessions on incorrigible rogues, vagabonds, and sturdy beggars; (2) by one justice on an offender convicted a third time of attending an illegal prayer-meeting; (3) by the justices of assize on the moss-troopers of Northumberland and Cumberland. The Act 18 Charles II. cap. 3, is to the effect that "benefit of clergy shall be taken away from great known and notorious thieves and spoil-takers in Northumberland and Cumberland, or otherwise that it shall be lawful for the justices of assize, etc., to transport, or cause to be transported, said offenders into any of His Majesty's dominions in America." This Act was continued by 17 Geo. II. till 24th January 1751. Persons on whom this punishment was inflicted were at first bound to transport themselves, under penalty of hanging if they failed to do so; but in this case, as it always will be, a heavy penalty does not compensate for uncertainty of detection, and it was soon found necessary to contract with some person to carry off the transported offenders, the contractor being remunerated by acquiring a right to the labour of the criminals for the duration of their sentences. The practice was legalised in 1717 by 4 Geo. I. cap. 2, an Act which authorised transportation as a substitute for other punishments besides that of hanging. The preamble and general tenor of this Act are to the following effect:—

That the present laws are not effectual to deter from crime; that many offenders to whom the royal mercy hath been extended upon condition of transporting themselves to the West Indies, have often neglected to perform the said condition, but returned to their former wickedness, and been at last for new crimes brought to a shameful ignominious death. And whereas, in many of His Majesty's colonies and plantations in America, there is great want of servants, etc., be it enacted . . . that any person convicted of any offence for which he is liable to be whipt or burnt on the hand, or shall have been ordered to any workhouse . . . may be sent to some of His Majesty's colonies and plantations in America. . . . And the court before whom he is convicted shall have power to convey, transport, or make over such offenders to any such person as shall contract for the performance of such transportation, and to his assigns, for such term of years as the Act empowers, and they shall have property and interest in the service of such person for such term of years. Offenders returning before expiration of term to be liable to death. The king may pardon an offender sentenced to such transportation, the offender paying his owner. Contractors to give security for performance of contract, and to obtain certificate from the governor of the colony of having fulfilled it.

Transportation was established, therefore, as a kind of slave trade, and offenders were put up to auction and sold for the period of their sentences by the person who had contracted to transport them. It is stated that, at one time, the rate was about £20 per head. Sometimes the contractor released them on payment of a sum of money, and it was said that some contractors who shipped their convicts at Bristol landed some of them on Lundy Island, a few miles down the channel.

It seems that the trade was not without its risks as a commercial speculation. The gaols in which the prisoners had been confined were so unwholesome, and probably the transport ships themselves so crowded and unclean, that the mortality in the cargo was sometimes very considerable. Howard, in his *State of Prisons*, referring to the many instances he had seen of prisoners' toes rotting from their feet, quotes a letter from Messrs. Stephenson and Randolf, of Bristol—great contractors for transport convicts—complaining of this to Mr. Biggs, gaoler at Salisbury, in a letter dated 13th September 1774, thus:—"Sore feet prove very fatal. The mortality we met with in our last ship, if repeated in this, will so surfeit us that we shall never take another. We lost an immense sum by them, and our ship is detained to this moment under quarantine." It appears also that some who were sentenced to transportation were detained in prison; for Howard mentions one man sentenced to transportation in 1774 who was still in Dolgelly gaol in 1782, others in Newcastle and Morpeth gaols in 1773-76. In course of time, also, the contractors found competitors in the African slave dealers, so that, in order to meet their risks, they demanded and received from the county local authorities a payment for each criminal they carried out. Howard, in his *State of Prisons*, gives the sum paid to each gaoler for expenses of conveyance from the prison, and payment "supposed" to be received by the contractor for transporting, which vary from a few shillings to twelve pounds per head, indicating that the practice was not uniform; but the expense seems to have all been borne by the local jurisdictions until the days of transportation to Australia, or till the establishment of the hulk system in England by 16 Geo. III. cap. 43, and following Acts, which enact that the expense of these establishments should be provided by Parliament.

The American colonies, especially Barbadoes, Maryland, and New York, steadily protested against their country being made the receptacle for outcasts of this description, and the propriety of sending them either to the East Indies or to Africa was discussed, but without result. Time arrived, however, in 1776, when the difficulty could no longer be postponed. The war of American independence, of course, put an end to transportation so far as that continent was concerned, for the Government did not think it proper to continue to the loyal colonies an infliction which they could no longer force the independent provinces to submit to. The Government of that day thus found themselves face to face with two problems of extreme difficulty, the solution of which did not readily present itself, and which, as the sequel will show, they succeeded only in postponing. The first problem was that of providing prison accommodation for the large number of prisoners—estimated by Mr. Eden, in 1778, to number 1000 annually—who henceforth could no longer be sent to the old penal settlements, and who would accumulate year by year till a vast total was reached. The second was that of so dealing with these accumulated outcasts, that either by fear of the punishment, or change of disposition, or in some other way, they should be as little dangerous to society in England, when the time came for their discharge, as they would be if they had been removed by transportation to a life of better opportunities and fewer temptations in the backwoods of America.

To solve the problem of providing prison accommodation, Acts of Parliament were passed enjoining the justices throughout the country to provide buildings for increased numbers in the bridewells or houses of correction—where it was proposed to place the criminals sentenced to transportation—and to retain them under severe discipline, as a separate class, and subject to hard work. To provide for the confinement of offenders pending the more permanent arrangements contemplated, 16 Geo. III. cap. 43 authorised their being imprisoned in hulks, and two old hulks at Woolwich were converted into prisons where convicts, employed in various works connected with the harbour, dockyard, and arsenal, might be lodged;[1] and, as the justices did not comply with the injunctions as to enlarging the houses of correction, additional hulks were afterwards provided at the other royal dockyards. The hulk system was established as a mere temporary expedient—the permanent system was (see 19 Geo. III. cap. 74) intended to be that of confining the prisoners in penitentiaries so built as to afford a separate cell to every inmate. In these penitentiaries they were to be compelled to labour in association, and to be subjected to religious and reformatory influences; and, if the penitentiary system had been adopted then instead of the hulk system, it is impossible to tell the amount of crime and corruption that would have been avoided, or the benefit that might have resulted both to England and her colonies. The course adopted, however, was that which is not unfrequently preferred when the choice lies between an easy temporary expedient and one involving difficulties in execution, though more permanently useful; and if, in addition to being easy, the temporary course has also the recommendation of being for the moment cheaper,

[1] They commenced the conversion of the Warren into the present Royal Arsenal at Woolwich. A newspaper of September 1777 says, in language which has no tinge of modern humanitarianism, "The place where the convicts are now at work is enclosing on the land side with a brick wall, so that spectators will soon (if not already) be barred the sight of those miserable wretches on the land side, except at a distance."

hardly any considerations of solid advantage will enable the better recommendation to prevail. The penitentiaries were not built, but the hulk system was continued, improved no doubt by subsequent Acts of Parliament. By 19 Geo. III. cap. 74 it was made a distinct punishment, which a court might inflict for certain crimes punishable by transportation; imprisonment in the hulks from one to five years being the equivalent of seven years' transportation, and (not exceeding) seven years in the hulks the equivalent of fourteen years' transportation.

The *temporary* expedient adopted in 1776 lasted between eighty and ninety years, for it was not finally put an end to in England until the burning of the *Defence* hulk at Woolwich, in July 1857, caused the removal of the convicts first to the *Unité* hospital ship at Woolwich, and afterwards to Lewes gaol in September of the same year, and ultimately the establishment of the invalid convict prison at Woking, in March 1860. In fact, it had its representative until the convict prison at Gibraltar was closed in 1875; for that prison was constructed after the model of a hulk prison, its hospital was a hulk, and many of the greatest evils of the hulks remained in full activity in it until the last. What the system must have been at its commencement and long after, the neglect or ignorance which must have prevailed throughout the whole arrangements, may be seen by reference to the official literature of those times. Howard called attention to the condition of the hulks as regards the health of the prisoners, and a public inquiry showed that between August 1776, when the convicts were first put on board the *Justicia*, and March 1778, out of 632 prisoners who had been received 176 had died. The population of this hulk in 1779 was 256; and, if this represents the average of the above years, the mortality was above 30 per cent per annum. Howard, in 1792, remarks the great improvements caused by this public inquiry; nevertheless, from July 12th 1776 to 12th December 1795, a period of nineteen and a half years, out of 7999 convicts sent to the hulks, 1946, or nearly one-fourth, died, mostly of "hulk fever." The inquiries thus set on foot in due course produced their fruit, though not, perhaps, as soon as could have been desired; but there is no doubt that in attention to sanitary construction and management prisons were many years in advance of any other institutions. As a contrast to the figures given above, it may be stated that the mortality in English convict prisons for males is now about 13 per 1000 per annum; that epidemics originating in the prisons have for many years been quite unknown, and that if any such disease finds its way in from outside, it is speedily arrested and disappears without spreading.

In regard to morals and discipline, it is difficult to realise anything worse than the hulk system must have been during a great part of its continuance. Every evil prevailed on board these prison ships that can be supposed to arise from the unchecked association of men of foul lives and unrestrained passions, with no more restraint than was enforced by gaolers of a very inferior class, with extremely imperfect ideas of discipline. The following extracts from the Report of the Committee of the House of Commons, in 1832, on secondary punishments, show clearly the state at which matters had arrived at that period:—

The great principles which your Committee have endeavoured to establish are the necessity of a separation of criminals, and of a severity of punishment sufficient to make it an object of terror to the evil-doer. In both these respects the system of management in the hulks is not only necessarily deficient, it is actually opposed to them. All that has been stated of the miserable effects of the association of criminals in the prisons on shore, the profaneness, the vice, the demoralisation, that are its inevitable consequences, applies in its fullest extent in the case now under consideration. The convicts, after being shut up for the night, are allowed to have lights between decks in some ships as late as ten o'clock; that, although against the rules of the establishment, they are permitted the use of musical instruments; that flash songs, dancing, fighting, and gaming take place; that the old offenders are in the habit of robbing the newcomers; that newspapers and improper books are clandestinely introduced; that a communication is frequently kept up with their old associates on shore, and that occasionally spirits are introduced on board. It is true that the greater part of these practices is against the rules of the establishment, but their existence in defiance of these rules shows an inherent defect in the system. The convicts are also permitted to receive visits from their friends, and, during the time they remain, are excused working, and it is stated that instances are frequent of their exemption from labour being extended to several days at the request of their friends. It is obvious that such communication must have the worst effect; it not only affords an indulgence to which no person in the situation of a convict is entitled, but it allows the most dangerous and improper intercourse to be kept up with old companions, from whom it is most important to disconnect them. The most assiduous attention on the part of the ministers of religion would be insufficient to stem the torrent of corruption flowing from these various and abundant sources; but, unless the evidence of these witnesses is utterly unworthy of belief, it appears that but little attention is paid to the promotion of religious feelings, or to the improvement of the morals of the convicts, and that, except for a short time on Sunday morning, the chaplains have no communication whatever with them.

The Committee are of opinion that too much money is placed at the disposal of the convicts; as, in addition to any which, on coming on board, they may conceal about their persons (and which it appears there is no difficulty in doing), and to what they may receive from their friends, an allowance is made out of the earnings of their labour of 3d. per day to those in the first class, and 1½d. to those in the second. Of this the convicts in the first class receive 6d., and those in the second 3d. per week, to lay out in the purchase of tea, tobacco, etc., and the remainder is reserved, and given to them when they are liberated from confinement.

This short sketch of the manner in which a criminal sentenced to transportation for crimes, to which the law affixes the penalty of death, passes his time, which portrays him well-fed, well-clothed, indulging in riotous enjoyment by night, with moderate labour by day, will prepare the House for readily believing that confinement on board the hulks fails to excite a proper feeling of terror in the minds of those who are likely to come under its operation. The minutes of evidence furnish ample testimony that the hulks are not dreaded; "that life in them is considered a pretty jolly life;" and that if a criminal can conquer the sense of shame which such degradation is calculated to excite, he is in a better situation than a large proportion of the working classes who have nothing but their daily labour to depend on for a subsistence.

It may be doubted whether, in the days when the hulk system existed, either the Parliament or the Government understood or felt their duties and responsibilities in the matter; but there can be no doubt that the arrangements they made contained no evidence that they either foresaw or cared to prevent the results which actually followed. The hulks were at first placed under the Local Justices; the overseer was appointed by them, and the other officers by the overseer; the maintenance of the establishment was committed to a contractor (£38 per annum per convict was the charge in 1776, which is actually much above the cost of a convict in these times), and, with reckless ignorance or indifference, the contractor was made overseer, carrying out, in fact, the idea of white slavery on which the previous transportation system had been founded. An Inspector of the hulks was provided for in the Act of Parliament, but was not appointed until 1802. His duty was to report to the Court of King's Bench, who evidently steadily neglected to exercise any control; and it was not till after successive encroachments on the part of the Secretary of State, ratified afterwards by Act of Parliament, that any direct control over these establishments was exercised at all on the part of Government. The Inspector was (1815) succeeded by a Superintendent of the hulks, who was in fact a clerk in the Secretary of State's office. This office was abolished in 1847, and for a short interval the duty of management of the hulks was performed by "a Person" with an unnamed office, until in 1850 the Board of Directors of Convict Prisons was constituted, under which all these institutions have since remained.

At the period when this fatal temporary expedient of hulks was adopted, an opportunity offered for reviving the transportation system in another continent, and under entirely different conditions. Fortunate would it have been if these differences had been so understood, and the science of penology so far advanced, that the system established could have been worked without the enormous evils which ultimately developed themselves. The first attempt made was to found a penal settlement in Sierra Leone, but this was abandoned very soon on account of the unsuitability of the climate to the European constitution. The eastern coast of Australia, which had been discovered by Cook in 1770 in his first voyage round the world, was next fixed on as the site of a new penal colony, and on the 13th of May 1787 the first expedition, taking 184 males and 100 females in four transports, started from Spithead under Commodore

Phillips, and arrived at Botany Bay after a voyage of eight months, including one spent at Rio. The settlement was actually formed at Port Jackson, about five miles from Botany Bay, 26th January 1788.

The average number transported yearly up to 1816 was only 474, the total number during those thirty years being 14,236. It is clear from the smallness of this number as compared with the number (1000) for whom Mr. Eden in 1778 estimated we should have to provide, and the numbers subsequently transported to New South Wales and Van Diemen's Land, which averaged in the next twenty-one years about 3000 per annum, and amounted in the year 1834 to 4920, that during these first thirty years our penal system was that of the hulks as much as that of transportation. Accumulation in the hulks was prevented by very freely remitting the sentences.

The Committee of 1838 thus speak of the new transportation system as compared with that which had existed previously:—

> The offenders who were transported in the past century to America were sent to communities, the bulk of whose population were men of thrift and probity; the children of improvidence were dropped in by driblets among the mass of a population already formed, and were absorbed and assimilated as they were dropped in.
>
> In New South Wales, on the contrary, the community was composed of the very dregs of society—of men proved by experience to be unfit to be at large in any society, and who were sent from the British gaols, and turned loose to mix with one another in the desert, together with a few taskmasters who were to set them to work in the open wilderness, and with the military who were to keep them from revolt.
>
> The consequences of this strange assemblage were vice, immorality, frightful disease, hunger, dreadful mortality among the settlers. The convicts were decimated by pestilence on the voyage,

and again decimated by famine on their arrival; and the most hideous cruelty was practised towards the unfortunate natives.

Such is the early history of New South Wales. Many of the evils certainly might have been provided against, whereas the evils of the hulk system were inherent in it and unpreventible. It has now been recognised that one of the most important and indispensable elements of proper prison discipline is a proper construction of the prison, and this could by no ingenuity be attained by any adaptation of an old hulk; and, moreover, the authorities in those days did not try. If they provided for the secure custody of the prisoners, they considered they had done all that was necessary; and they did not attain any remarkable success even in this department. A review of the transportation system as it was actually carried out for many years shows clearly that the only ideas which prevailed among those who framed and carried out the system were (1) to get rid of the convict as cheaply as possible, or to keep him as profitably in a pecuniary point of view, and with as little expenditure as possible; (2) to make the punishment as deterrent as severity could make it, and as the human frame could endure. The very notion of reformation seems hardly to have entered into the thoughts of anybody able to give effect to it. The results produced by this kind of treatment, as shown by the condition to which it brought those who were subject to it, would be hardly credible if they did not stand officially recorded on the most indubitable testimony; and it will serve a useful purpose to record them now, because from time to time we see a tendency to undervalue reformatory influences, and to rely solely on severity and repression in dealing with our criminals—a feeling which perhaps may take its rise from a natural reaction produced by the idea that an exaggerated sentimentality has in its turn prevailed in our system of punishment.

The penitentiary system, which, as has been stated above, was in 1779 decided on as that which should be definitely established, did not emerge from the region of talk until Millbank Prison was built (1816 to 1821) after an expenditure of £458,000. Imprisonment in the penitentiary was, like imprisonment in the hulks, at first intended as a separate sentence instead of transportation; they both became subsequently places for the confinement of prisoners under sentence of transportation, in some cases serving there the whole period of punishment (which was not by any means the whole period of the sentence, for an irregular system of pardons was instituted with a view to shortening the periods of detention to those laid down in 1779 as equivalent to various terms of transportation), in others making there only a stay of greater or less duration previous to the voyage to the antipodes. Those who were destined to the latter fate were put for the voyage on board a convict ship, in which, from the nature of the case, they were all mixed up in close contact and companionship, with the most imperfect supervision; and here, of course, commenced the process of mutual corruption, which necessarily followed from the scarcely restrained intercourse of persons the majority of whom were of depraved or evil habits.

The following description of life in a convict ship on its voyage out to Australia is derived from an account of what occurred on board the *Hillsborough*, in which Dr. Vanderkemp, with three Moravian missionaries, sailed in 1798 for New South Wales:—

> About 240 of these miserable creatures were chained in pairs, hand to hand or leg to leg, with no light but what came in at the hatchways. At first the darkness of the place, the rattling of the chains, and the dreadful imprecations of the prisoners, suggested ideas of the most horrid nature, and combined to form a lively picture of the infernal regions. Besides, in a short time a putrid fever broke out among the convicts, and carried off 34 before the ship reached the Cape, and the ship became loathsome beyond description.

It was long indeed before the Government recognised its duty to provide every convict ship with a religious instructor or catechist, an improvement first made by Sir James Graham on the suggestion of the Bishop of London (Blomfield). Bibles were furnished for the use of the prisoners, no doubt, but they were not apparently always turned to exactly the purpose they were intended for. On one occasion the convicts were found to have procured a pack of cards to beguile the time, and it turned out that these cards were made by pasting together several leaves of the Bibles, and the artist who designed the court cards had managed to make the four knaves into excellent likenesses of the captain and other superior officers. While mentioning the riot and dissipation of which these ships were the scene, it is fair to recall one remarkable instance in which the convicts gave most welcome support to authority—viz. on the occasion when the convict guard of Irish soldiers rose in mutiny and attempted to take the ship, when the convicts were actually armed, and kept the guard in custody until the arrival of the ship in some place where authority could be established.

When the first consignment of convicts went to New South Wales in 1787 their labour was of course devoted to raising crops for their own future sustenance, constructing the necessary buildings, and making a commencement of opening up the country. A few of them were set free and received grants of land. An expedition was also sent to Norfolk Island, with a view to growing flax, and subsequently 200 convicts were sent there. This station was abandoned on account of the difficulty of landing there, and the prisoners removed to Van Diemen's Land, but in 1824 re-established as a penal settlement. To Van Diemen's Land, at the mouth of the Derwent, were also removed the convicts who had been sent to form a settlement at Point Nepean, Port Phillip, in 1803, which it had become necessary to abandon on account of the badness of the situation selected by Colonel Collins, who founded it. It is recorded that, during the short time the settlement existed, some of the prisoners escaped; one named Buckley was never retaken, but he reappeared in 1835, after thirty-two years' wandering among the blacks, having forgotten his own language. The necessity for providing fresh settlements for the large numbers of convicts who were sent out, and perhaps a desire to forestall the French by taking possession of all parts of the continent, led, in 1826, to the formation of a penal station at King George's Sound under Major Lockyer; but this was abandoned in 1829. The convicts as a body were idle and negligent; they quarrelled with and ill-used the natives, and some endeavoured to escape inland, under the impression that they would be able to walk to China. The hand of the Government fell heavily on those who disturbed the order of the community, whether convicts or free men. Six soldiers were hanged at one time for making a false key to open a store, and a convict was flogged for pretending to have discovered a gold mine. Whether this was altogether a pretence, or whether rather he may not have merely failed to prove his alleged discovery to the satisfaction of the authorities, is, with our present knowledge of the richness of the colony in gold, a fair subject of doubt. When subsequently a certain number of free persons began to establish themselves by emigration to the colony, and to become employers of labour, a system was introduced of assigning the convicts to these employers as practically their slaves. A decision of the judges in New South Wales, founded on 9 Geo. IV. cap. 83, s. 9, established that the assignee had a freehold in the person of the convict, and that the Government could not arbitrarily revoke the assignment. A portion, however, were still retained in the service of the Government for the execution of public works, roads, etc., and, as the system developed, a portion were sent to "penal settlements," in which those who were considered exceedingly bad characters were detained under a more severe and repressive discipline.

In giving an account of the manner in which transportation was carried out in the Australian colonies, it would be very tedious and not very practicable to describe in detail all the variations embodied in the successive regulations. Each governor who came out to rule the settlement seems to have modified the arrangements according to his own ideas; some were exceedingly severe, others leant to mildness and humanity.

Few probably, if any, had any experience before taking up their duties, and they were without that control or assistance which arises from a well-regulated and instructed public opinion. To these causes, as well as to the difficulties of the situation and the diversion of attention caused by the great war, must be attributed many of those regulations and arrangements which we now know to have been mistakes, and to have led at last to the great increase of crime, and the scandals reported from the colony which forced the matter on the attention of the public and the Government. One doctrine, which certainly struck at the root of the attempt to found a well-regulated community, was that which was laid down by Governor Macquarie, in 1809, that the colony was founded for the sake of the convicts and not for emigrants, and that therefore the former should be entirely on an equal footing with the latter. The two classes were therefore encouraged to associate socially together; the ex-convicts were placed in situations of trust, such as jurymen and even magistrates; and other situations in which character should be of the first importance were filled by the "emancipist" class, such as schoolmasters, clerks in public offices, police, etc.

The system must have been very costly, for in 1810, by which time only 9000 convicts had been sent out to New South Wales, the total population of the colony was only 10,500, of which 7000 were still convicts, and 4000 persons were still fed wholly or partly from the public stores. Up to this time the employers of labour were few, and the demand for labour therefore much below the supply of convicts who had to be disposed of, and it was therefore found necessary to tempt settlers to take convicts as their assigned servants by the grant of certain indulgences, such as free gifts of land in proportion to the number of convicts assigned. About that time, however, the suitability of the colony for wool-growing became established. The peace of 1815 enabled men to direct their time, attention, and money to projects of emigration; and in course of time the colonists became so desirous of obtaining the services of the convicts, that the assignment of a valuable convict became a matter of solicitation of the authorities, and led to jobbing and favour which was not put an end to till about 1835. Sir G. Arthur in Van Diemen's Land superseded the Board who had till then conducted the assignment, and appointed a sworn commission to act under distinct regulations framed to ensure the fair working of the system. Until employers could be found for the convicts, the males were retained in barracks, the females in penitentiaries, and employed for the public benefit; and Sir George Arthur instituted a plan of retaining the most valuable servants, such as mechanics, in the hands of Government, and hiring them out, for the profit of the public, to private employers. Those convicts who came out with very bad characters were also retained by Government, and not allowed at once the advantages of assignment. The convicts unassigned were ultimately divided into six classes, according to their character and conduct, the highest enjoying some partial liberty, the lowest working in irons and in the penal settlements.

On the satisfactory fulfilment of a certain period of servitude on assignment or in Government employment, a convict could receive a ticket-of-leave, by which he became virtually free in the colony for the rest of his sentence, but was under certain restrictions, such as being confined to a certain district, unless he received a pass to go out of it, being obliged to muster yearly or quarterly, being prohibited from carrying firearms, except by special permission, etc. This indulgence was first legalised by 9 Geo. IV. cap. 83, the granting of tickets-of-leave previously being merely a regulation of the Government, and not sanctioned by any positive law; and it was regulated by 2 & 3 Will. IV. cap. 62, s. 2, which enacted that the least period in which it could be gained was by serving four years for a sentence of seven years, six years for a sentence of fourteen years, and eight years for a sentence for life, in assigned service or Government employment; but these periods could be increased by misconduct of any kind. Free pardons were also granted to a fourteen years' man after two-thirds of his sentence had expired, and to a life man after twelve years. An application by a convict who had held a ticket-of-leave for six years without interruption, with good conduct, and who was recommended by respectable people in the colony, was usually transmitted for the gracious allowance of the Crown. It may be inferred from an answer given by Sir R. Bourke (see App. C, No. 41, p. 234 of the *Report* of 1838), that, before the regulation of the periods of service laid down in the above Act, the convicts were granted tickets-of-leave to some extent, at the discretion of the Government, and on application from "influential persons in England."

The assigned servants were required to live under

their employer's roof, were not allowed to work for themselves, or to be out at night, or to go anywhere without a pass. It is clear that these rules were not enforced, for convicts were allowed to go and lodge in Hobart Town for three or four days in the week on condition of working for the master for the remainder; and the masters in some cases encouraged them to evil courses by allowing them entire freedom on condition of their bringing them from time to time a share of any money they could gain. The employers were not bound to do more than provide them with the necessities of life, in the way of food, clothing, etc., on a very liberal scale. To those whose services they were especially desirous of retaining, they found it necessary, however, to give some wages and indulgences, besides shutting their eyes to their irregularities and those assigned servants who had no wages considered themselves entitled to compensate themselves by pilfering from their masters.

It is clear that to these men the punishment of a sentence of transportation consisted simply in their being converted into slaves to a private employer—for such they were—differing only from slaves of the ordinary kind, that their master had only a temporary and personal property in them, and that he could not punish them himself, but must complain to a magistrate, who could order them to be flogged or condemned to work on the roads, or in the chain gang, or otherwise dealt with. A single magistrate had power to order 150 lashes until 1833, when he was limited to 50. "In 1834 the number of convicts in Van Diemen's Land was about 15,000, the summary convictions amounted to about 15,000, and the number of lashes inflicted was about 50,000. On the other hand, a convict, if ill treated, may complain of his master, and if he substantiate his charge, his master is deprived of his services; but for this purpose the convict must go before a bench, sometimes one hundred miles distant, composed of magistrates, most of whom are owners of convict labour. Legal redress is therefore rarely sought for, and still more rarely obtained by the injured convict." The employers, however, did not find corresponding difficulties in getting the law enforced against their convict servants. On the contrary, the facility they enjoyed is exemplified in the story of a convict having been sent with a note requesting that the magistrate would be kind enough to order him to be flogged and returned.

It is curious to contrast the figures which represent the convict population of the country about that period and at the present time and the amount of corporal punishment found necessary to keep them under control. The convict population of Great Britain, with its population of about 15,000,000, then consisted of 43,000 convicts in New South Wales and Van Diemen's Land, besides others in the penal settlements; the convicts in ten hulks in Great Britain, of which the usual number was stated in 1828 to be 3000 or 4000; several hundreds in the penitentiary at Millbank; about 900 (in 1838) at Gibraltar, and probably as many or more at Bermuda, about 50,000 in all. This large number is represented now by less than 9000 from our population of nearly 27,000,000 to whom should be added, say, 2000 on ticket-of-leave. The corporal punishments inflicted among all these prisoners number on an average 72 per annum, which is to be compared with the 158,000 lashes assigned by the Committee of 1838 as the number inflicted in one year in New South Wales and Van Diemen's Land. It may be added that the executions in New South Wales, on an average of the ten years ending with 1837, amounted to 65 free and 26·2 bond persons, out of a population which numbered, in 1836, 77,096, of which 25,254 were male, and 2577 female convicts, or 327 in the whole of the ten years.

Two fatal evils attended the assignment system, from the very necessity of the case. First, the result on the character of the employer of having almost despotic power over the persons of his fellow men and women, evinced, as stated by Sir R. Bourke, in an insolent, uncharitable, imperious, haughty, and violent conduct, approaching to inhumanity. Second, the corresponding moral result on the convict, and the great inequalities in the degree of punishment each individual suffered, varying, as it must have done, with the character of the employer, the position of the convict with regard to him, and the nature of the employment he was put to. The system had separate and special evils with regard to the women convicts. Being mostly of depraved characters originally, their vicious propensities cultivated and developed in the transport ships and the factories or penitentiaries, where they lived in free association, and exposed on their release from prison to temptations and opportunities which it was almost impossible for them to resist, they became irredeemably profligate for the most part; the respectable settlers avoided receiving them as assigned servants; and they came, therefore, into the hands of the lower class, many being, it was said, notoriously maintained as prostitutes. Other evil results attended the system, not from being inherent to it, but from the manner in which it was carried out, and its intention evaded. It was said to be well understood before 1832 that convicts sentenced to transportation arranged that, shortly after arriving in the colony, they should be assigned to persons with whom they had an understanding, and became, in fact, their masters. One flagrant case illustrates this point. A man was transported for robbing a bank. The plunder was successfully concealed, though the man was taken. His wife brought it out with her, the convict was assigned to her as a servant, and the intended punishment for his crime became, of course, a most successful investment of the proceeds of it.

Convicts who offended against the laws or regulations of the colony might be sentenced to work on the roads with or without irons, or to be transported to a penal settlement. There were several of these places at various times, as at Newcastle, Port Macquarie, etc., but in 1838 there were only two for New South Wales, viz., Norfolk Island for men only, where in 1837 there were 1200, and Moreton Bay for males and females, which contained, in 1837, 300. The penal settlements for Van Diemen's Land were Norfolk Island, Macquarie Harbour, and Tasman's Peninsula, or Port Arthur, where there were, in 1835, 1173 convicts, and there had been others, which were abandoned about 1833. At these places they were not assigned as servants (except a few for the Government officers), but were kept at severe labour, felling trees, making roads, etc., in single or double irons. For a long time but one idea seems to have prevailed in the management of these settlements, viz. that of grinding severity. No appeal was made to the moral feelings, no hope held out to the convict, no religious feeling awakened or instilled into him. Mere brute force alone was relied on; and, with a fatally mistaken view of economy, convicts were employed as overseers—men, no doubt, generally of low moral tone, who could not gain that peculiar influence which is exerted by those for whom a respect can be entertained. Removal to these places came, therefore, to be much dreaded. The extreme severity, and the disorders and crimes of the foulest nature which were committed there, aroused such horror among the convicts themselves, and their condition appeared to them so hopeless, that Sir R. Bourke stated that he had abundant reasons to suspect that capital crimes had been committed on Norfolk Island, from a desperate determination to stake the chance of capital conviction and punishment in Sydney against the chances of escape which the passage might afford to the accused or to the witnesses.[1] To remove this motive a criminal court was established in the island. Unnatural crime prevailed so extensively in Norfolk Island that Sir G. Gipps estimated that one-eighth of the whole were guilty of it; and Mr. Mackonochie could not put the proportion lower than one-thirtieth. Murder seems also to have been rife, so that a discharged convict replied to a question about a certain murder: "*I have seen so many that I do not know which you refer to. I have seen men cut up in barracks just as you would cut up meat.* I have seen 21 men executed

[1] See *Report*, 1832, p. 30.

in a fortnight" for murders committed at Moreton Bay, brought on by the severity of the system under which they were treated.

More direct methods of procuring their release from these places were of course attempted. Several mutinies occurred at the penal settlements, in which officers and prisoners were killed. Norfolk Island was, about 1826, taken by convicts. In 1834 another mutiny took place, in which 9 convicts were killed, and 11 subsequently executed. The Rev. Dr. Ullathorne says that when he went into the gaol and announced the names of those who were to die, one after another, as their names were pronounced, dropped on their knees and thanked God that they were to be delivered from that horrible place, the others standing mute. The fatal effect of attempting to escape does not seem to have entirely prevented endeavours to do so. From the formation of the establishment at Macquarie Harbour, 3d January 1822 to 16th May 1827, there were 116 such attempts. Of these 75 were supposed to have perished in the woods, 1 was hanged for murdering and eating his companion, 2 were shot by the military, 8 are known to have been murdered, and 6 *eaten by their companions*, 24 escaped to the settled districts, 13 of whom were hanged for bushranging, and 2 for murder, making 101 of the 116 who came to an untimely end.

As the idea of reforming the convicts does not seem to have entered into the minds of those who framed the transportation system, and as no chaplains seem to have been appointed even to the hulks till after 1802, it is not very surprising that no kind of provision was made for religious ministrations or instruction to those who were first sent out; but, as the expedition to Botany Bay in 1787 was on the point of sailing, an appeal was made to those in authority, and, through the intercession of the Bishop of London, the Rev. Richard Johnson was appointed chaplain. No church or chapel was built, however, for six years; and so little did those in authority consider it their duty to set any example in attending service, that it was not until 1825, after an attempt to enforce attendance by a system of duress and punishment had failed to bring more than five or six persons together for the purpose, that the Governor, Sir R. Darling, began regularly, with his lady and family, to attend divine worship on Sundays. Up to 1807 there was only one chaplain for the settlements, excepting for six years out of the nineteen, when there were two, and in 1803 a Roman Catholic priest, who was a convict, was set free to enable him to exercise his clerical functions. Many of the road parties and chain gangs were visited only occasionally by a chaplain, and some not at all. Till the year 1836 the settlement of Norfolk Island had never been visited by a chaplain except once in 1791.

In 1836 this subject engaged the serious attention of the authorities, both in the colonies and in England, and in consequence Acts were passed to facilitate the building of churches and chapels and the appointment of ministers, and the Home Government took on itself its share of the expense of paying and sending out ministers and schoolmasters of various denominations, to provide for the spiritual and educational care of the population for whom they were responsible.

The alarming increase of crime, which, measured by the number of criminals convicted, had doubled between

1817 and 1831, led to the appointment of a Committee of the House of Commons in the latter year. As it appeared from their investigations that transportation was not sufficiently dreaded as a punishment; orders were given by Mr. Stanley, in 1833, that in future all hardened criminals should serve a large portion of their sentences either in a penal settlement or in a road gang before being assigned to private service, and that the class of "gentleman convicts," whose prosperous condition was thought to be an incentive to crime through the reports of it which reached England, should all be sent to penal settlements, so that they might not escape punishment by the collusive arrangements for their assignment already referred to.

The Committee of 1838 entirely condemned the system of transportation as it had been carried on, as being unequal, without terrors to the criminal class, corrupting to both convict and colonist, and very expensive; and they recommended punishment in penitentiaries instead. Lord Glenelg began by modifying the system of transportation and assignment, directing that all convicts should first pass through the course of penal labour in labour gangs, and that none should be assigned for domestic service or for purposes of mere luxury. The Government also decided that a larger proportion of the duration of the sentence should be passed in this country, to send more convicts to Bermuda (a mere hulk establishment, formed in 1824, and not a place in which convicts were assigned or discharged at the end of their sentences, as in Australia), and to try and improve the discipline in New South Wales and Van Diemen's Land. In 1840 transportation to New South Wales was stopped entirely, and in 1842 a convict (hulk) establishment was opened at Gibraltar, as an addition to the means of retaining convicts, under control, on Government works before sending them to make their own living in Australia.

In 1842 Lord Stanley framed the improved system which was intended thenceforth to be followed, in which assignment of convicts had no place whatever. It was termed the Probation System, and was based on the idea of passing convicts through various stages of control and discipline, by which it was hoped a progressive reform would be effected in them, and a desire to do well stimulated by ensuring that such conduct should be followed by improvement in their condition. The first stage was the probation gang in Van Diemen's Land, through which all convicts transported were to pass, with the exception of a few who will be referred to. These gangs were scattered over the colony, and employed on public works, under the control of Government, wherever their services might be required. A schoolmaster or a clergyman was to be attached to each. From thence the convict passed into the stage of probation pass, during which he might, with consent of Government, engage in private service for wages, but, according as their conduct had been in the probation gangs, they were required to pay in to Government a part or the whole of their earnings, to be retained as a security, and to be forfeited if the pass-holder misconducted himself, and they were subjected to other restrictions giving them only a modified liberty. The next stage was that of ticket-of-leave, which gave the same privileges as under the assignment system.

The last stage was that of a conditional pardon. But for convicts of whom greater hopes of reformation were entertained, and for those who, on the other hand, were considered of deeper criminality, other stages were added. The first, comprising selected men of not more than seven years' sentence, were to pass a preliminary period, not exceeding eighteen months, in a penitentiary in this country, and, according to their conduct in this stage, to be placed on their arrival in Australia in either a probation gang, or on probation pass, or on ticket-of-leave. The convicts under life sentences, or those whose crimes were of an aggravated nature, and who had been sentenced to fifteen years or more, were to commence with the penal discipline of Norfolk Island.

Pentonville Prison was opened in December 1842 to afford means (with Millbank) of applying that part of the system which was to be carried out in England.

The probation system was, in principle, a great advance on anything that had been done before. It made a great step towards establishing the separation of the prisoners while under punishment, which is the foundation of our penal system, and, besides recognising the necessity of moral and religious teaching, it laid down rules for general and systematic application, founded on the idea of encouraging convicts to self-restraint and good behaviour—it appealed generally to higher feelings than fear, and endeavoured to secure discipline by other means than severity and brute force. It also introduced a certainty into the amount of punishment which any convict would undergo, which was entirely wanting in the assignment system. But it had hardly been founded before it broke down from two causes—one, that suitable means had not been provided for ensuring proper order in the probation gangs. They were herded together in huts under conditions which resembled sufficiently that of the prisoners in the hulks to ensure the same evils prevailing in them. The officers in charge of the gangs were of inferior qualifications, a large number were convicts, and, on the whole, these gangs were characterised by insolence, insubordination and prevailing vice, unnatural crime being proved to exist to a terrible extent. The other was that the demand for labour in the colony was found to be quite insufficient to enable the "probation pass" and "ticket-of-leave" stages to be carried into effect, and this difficulty reacted on and increased extremely the one above referred to; for it became necessary to establish "hiring gangs," in which the convicts were maintained by Government and employed on Government works until they could find masters, and in these, of course, the evils of the probation gangs prevailed to an equal degree. The stations, no doubt, varied in degrees of badness, but some descended so low that Governor Latrobe could describe them as distinguished by "utter abandonment of all order and decency."

Under this condition of things it became very doubtful whether the new system was really any improvement on the old, for assignment, as was argued, at least secured the advantage of dispersion of most of the convicts, with the chance that many would fall into good hands and adopt a respectable mode of life, whereas the gangs became nurseries of vice, and the moral and religious teaching which was rendered possible by their being kept together was quite counteracted by the condition in which they lived; nor were the religious teachers of a sufficiently high order for the work they had to perform.

Other evils arose from the details of the working of the system. Orders were given that the gangs were not to be employed on works of merely colonial or local advantage unless the colony paid for them, which they did not care to do. It became therefore exceedingly difficult to find employment for the convicts at all, and the gangs therefore became characterised by "excessive idleness." The arrangements also by which it was intended to ensure the Government retaining more control over the passholders, viz. allowing only short engagements, etc., were found troublesome by the employers, and therefore created an additional obstacle in the way of their finding private situations. A new system, such as this was, required, in short, to be developed gradually; but so far was this advantage from being secured, that the numbers poured into Van Diemen's Land during the five years ending with 1845 amounted to nearly 17,637, more than double the number sent in the previous five years, and the provision of suitable buildings (that all-important necessity in dealing with convicts) or the securing of efficient officers, who could not possibly fulfil their duties without some training, especially under the new ideas of endeavouring to reform the convict, was, of course, impossible. The emergency created by this failure in the anticipations on which the probation system was founded was so great that it was necessary to adopt temporary means of fulfilling the promises held out to those convicts who had been selected for the training of

Pentonville; and the best conducted men were sent to Port Phillip and New South Wales as exiles, instead of with tickets-of-leave to Van Diemen's Land. The consignments of 1670 sent to New South Wales in 1849 were the last which that colony has received.

In 1846 it was decided by Mr. Gladstone that, at all events, transportation to Van Diemen's Land must be suspended, to give time for recovery from the existing evils and for deliberation on the future, and it was accordingly suspended throughout 1847 and part of 1848. At first the formation of a new convict colony in North Australia was contemplated; but this project was abandoned, and in the beginning of 1847 another most important step was taken in the formation of our penal system. The discipline and moral training of the separate system had been found so efficacious by those to whom it had been applied in Pentonville as to cause observations to be made by the surgeons-superintendent of the convict ships which took them out to Australia on the tractability and good conduct they displayed during the voyage, and to cause very favourable reports to be sent home regarding them after taking up their abode in the colonies. It was determined therefore by Lord Grey, in conjunction with Sir George Grey, that every convict should undergo the first part of his sentence in a penitentiary at home, where strict separation, with industrial employment and moral training (on the plan adopted in Pentonville), should be enforced; that he should then be removed to a prison, either in England or at Gibraltar or Bermuda, where he should be employed on public works, such as the construction of harbours of refuge or works under some public department, for a further period of his sentence; and that he should then be transferred to a colony, with a ticket-of-leave, free to obtain employment for himself on his own terms (subject only to certain police restrictions), and ultimately obtaining a pardon conditional on his not returning to the country in which he was convicted.

The essence of the change introduced by the "probation system" was that certain portions of every sentence of transportation should be passed in a Government prison (of one kind or another, for the "gangs" must be considered as prisons), where it was intended the convict should suffer certain definite penal discipline, and be subjected to improving moral influences; during the remainder he was to be able to hire himself out or employ himself for his own advantage, subject to supervision, with a view to ensure his adoption of habits of honesty, good behaviour, and industry. The change made in 1847 was, first, that the whole of the convicts under sentence were to pass through the Pentonville system of training; and, secondly, that the other part of the penal stage of the sentence of transportation, viz. that which was passed on public works, was to be carried out in this country, thus ensuring the services of people fully qualified to carry out and superintend the arrangements efficiently, and bringing to bear on them the wholesome check and support of an educated public opinion. The establishments at Gibraltar and Bermuda did not fulfil these requirements, and so far interfered with the completeness of the arrangements. The convicts were to be sent to the colonies only after going through all this discipline and arriving at the stage of ticket-of-leave. In order to ensure suitable employment for those who could not at once be absorbed into private service, the Imperial Government consented to allow colonial works to be executed by the convicts without payment, and in order to counteract the demoralisation of the community which was alleged to result from flooding the colony with large numbers of convicts, principally adult males, the Imperial Government consented to devote the land revenue to purposes of emigration. A fund formed by requiring every convict to pay back to Government £15 towards the cost of his passage before receiving his conditional pardon, was devoted to the same purpose, and assistance was given towards sending out the wives and families of convicts.

It is obvious that the successful working of these arrangements depended on the possibility of the ticket-of-leave men being absorbed into private employment on their removal from this country. A transfer to Australia had come to be considered by very many rather as an advantage than a punishment, and it was held out in the regulations of the prisons at home as an inducement to good behaviour. But transfer from a public works prison at home to a road gang in Van Diemen's Land would be no privilege; and, moreover, so long as they remained on the hands of Government, a heavy charge fell on the public on account of them. In view, therefore, of the probability that Van Diemen's Land could not absorb all who would be sent out, various other colonies were invited to receive the ticket-of-leave men. The Report of the Committee of 1838, dilating on the results transportation had had on the community of New South Wales, had by this time, however, produced such an effect, that it was considered a stigma to be a "convict colony." The difference between forming a new community almost entirely from the convict class, without any attempt at previously disciplining or reforming them, as had been done in the case of New South Wales, and the new proposal of sending out persons who had been subjected to strict training and discipline to take their places amongst an already existing moral and well-ordered community, did not avail to induce the colonies to cooperate with this country in the plan. Even New South Wales, after much discussion and correspondence, finally declined to receive any more convicts on any conditions, and the Cape of Good Hope actually resisted (to the point of incipient rebellion) the landing of 300 convicts who were sent thither from Bermuda in the ship *Neptune* in 1850, in anticipation of the colony consenting (or, at all events, not objecting) to absorb such a small number. Western Australia alone, which, after struggling for twenty years, was now, with only 6000 inhabitants, in a state of utter stagnation, such as the discoveries of gold in the other Australian colonies in 1850 would in all likelihood have soon developed into extinction, almost unanimously petitioned that convicts might be sent thither, as their only chance of obtaining a supply of labour, and no doubt with a view to the benefits they would receive from the Government expenditure.

Concurrently with these steps, measures were taken to improve the condition of things among the probation gangs in Van Diemen's Land. The temporary suspension of transportation allowed many of the pass-holders to be absorbed and dispersed in private employment—no doubt the discovery of gold in Australia made room for the employment of more—and by this means a diminution of the number of gangs and a reduction and weeding of the staff of officers of the convict establishments became possible. The gangs were also lodged in buildings admitting of a proper separation of the convicts, and thus unnatural crime was checked. Ample and suitable employment was found so soon as the Home Government undertook to allow of the employment of convicts on colonial works without charge, and a system of taskwork was devised to ensure due industry in the gangs. Possibly, therefore, the system might thenceforward have worked beneficially to all concerned in it; but the feelings aroused in Van Diemen's Land by the revelations of the years preceding 1846 were so strong and deep that nothing short of an entire discontinuance of transportation would satisfy its inhabitants. In this they were supported by the neighbouring colonies, and the result was the formation of an "Australian League," pledged to oppose by all possible means the introduction of convicts into any part of Australia.

At the moment when the feeling of the colonists took this decided turn, the discovery of gold came to add force to their arguments by rendering it more than doubtful whether any punishment could be considered deterrent of which an important part consisted in removing the offender to that part of the world whither so many stirring and enterprising men were bending their steps with the assurance of thereby bettering their position. In 1852, then, transportation to Van

Diemen's Land ceased altogether, and thenceforward the only outlet for those convicts who had passed through the preliminary stages of their sentences was Western Australia.

The system followed out in Western Australia was that laid down in 1847, with one slight modification, viz. that a certain number of prisoners passed about a half of the "public works" period of their sentences in the colony. The ticket-of-leave men were dispersed over the country wherever they could find employers; those who were unable to do so were maintained, at the cost of the Imperial Government, in hiring depots or stations established in all the districts of the colony, and they were employed, after they had put up the buildings for their own accommodation, in making roads, building bridges, and generally executing such public works as the colony required. Each of these establishments or stations had the pastoral care of a chaplain, payment being made for the services both of Protestant and Roman Catholic ministers for this purpose. A large permanent cellular prison was built at Freemantle for those convicts who had not arrived at their ticket-of-leave stage; the other buildings were principally of a temporary character, in which the men lived in association and slept in hammocks. Latterly, in order to promote the execution of public works for the benefit of the colony, prisoners were sent to these road parties before arriving at the ticket-of-leave stage of their sentence. In order that the free community might not be gradually swamped by the convict element, and with a view to counteracting the evils likely to arise from the introduction of a preponderating number of adult males (for no female convicts were ever sent to Western Australia, in accordance with the strongly expressed desire of the colonists), the Home Government engaged to send out as many free persons to the colony as it did convicts; but the intention of this provision was frustrated, and the difficulty of making transportation an essential part of our penal system, *under the conditions which had now come to be acknowledged as necessary*—viz. that the convict element should not be allowed to predominate in the colony—was manifest when it was seen that not only the free inhabitants of the colony, who were there when convicts were first sent out, but also large numbers of the free immigrants sent out by the Government, shortly left the colony, attracted by the higher gains and greater opportunities presented by the gold fields and the more thriving communities of the other Australian colonies, where the value of their labour was not kept down by the competition of the imported criminals. It is indeed obvious that an importation of convicts to a colony is inconsistent with a concurrent free immigration; for the only object a colony can have in receiving convicts is to obtain cheap labour, and if this object is attained, there is no longer any inducement to free immigration of the labouring class, who must comprise the great bulk of the settlers.

As a convict settlement, Western Australia in all other respects answered perfectly, and proved the soundness of the principles embodied in the rules above referred to as having been laid down by Lord Grey and Sir George Grey in 1847. The community is as well ordered and law-abiding as the mother country; bushranging has never existed; life and property are perfectly safe; and there has been no suspicion of the prevalence of the crime which formed such a serious blot in the history of transportation in the other colonies.

## CHAPTER VI.

### PENAL SERVITUDE.

TRANSPORTATION continued for some years longer to form a part of our penal system; but from the time when Van Diemen's Land ceased to receive convicts, it no longer formed the foundation of it, but became only an adjunct of no very considerable importance.

When Western Australia was made a penal settlement, it might no doubt have been anticipated that settlers with capital at command might have come to take advantage of the supply of cheap labour, and that shortly the capacity of the colony for absorbing convicts would have increased up to the number to be furnished; but the discovery of gold in New South Wales and Victoria in 1850 diverted the whole stream of emigration to those colonies, and the prospects of Western Australia becoming, within a reasonable time, capable of serving as the only outlet for our convicts became more than doubtful. The mistake made in Van Diemen's Land, of pouring into the colony numbers far beyond its powers of absorption, was not, of course, repeated in Western Australia, and it was seen that the number that that colony could dispose of was very limited. Nor could the field for employment be kept open by the departure of men whose sentences had expired to the other colonies of Australia; for these latter passed stringent Acts for the prevention of the immigration of any person who had come out from Great Britain in the condition of a convict. Under these circumstances numerous proposals were made for the formation of a new convict colony, and many unoccupied islands and countries were suggested for the purpose. But this would obviously have been inconsistent with the principles which, after such a lengthened experience, had been laid down as essential in carrying out this mode of punishment. So long as convicts were in prison or in the hands of Government, they might of course be either in a prison at home or in a prison in a new colony (though experience showed that they would be managed better and certainly at much less cost if this stage were passed at home); but when the time came for them to be discharged from prison either on ticket-of-leave or expiration of sentence, a new settlement would afford little, if any, prospect of their finding employment or occupation. And even if this difficulty could be surmounted, we should have found ourselves again establishing a community of which the preponderating and overwhelming elements would consist of people of the low moral type who compose the criminal class. To enter on such a course as this in opposition to all the teachings of experience, could not of course be thought of, and new arrangements therefore had to be devised, based on the necessity for retaining all or most of our convicts in this country after the expiration of their sentences.

Thus was originated the Act of 1853, which allowed

the substitution of a sentence of Penal Servitude, which might be carried out in England, for all crimes punishable by transportation for less than fourteen years, it being supposed that Western Australia could absorb most of the convicts of the longer sentences. The sentences of penal servitude authorised by this Act were shorter than the sentences of transportation they replaced, as they were intended to correspond to the periods usually passed in prison by a convict under a sentence of transportation. A term as low as three years' penal servitude was authorised, and the practice of remitting part of the sentence by ticket-of-leave was abolished. In 1857 this Act was amended by legalising penal servitude for any crimes which might be punished by transportation, and in order that the invaluable influence obtained by enabling prisoners to gain on system a certain remission of their sentences might not be lost, the length of sentences by this Act was restored to correspond with the old sentences of transportation, on the understanding that a corresponding period of remission on ticket-of-leave might be granted. Transportation thenceforward became no longer a necessary mode of carrying out any sentence, and in deference mainly to the repeated and urgent wishes of the eastern colonies of Australia, no consignment of convicts has been sent to Western Australia since the year 1867. In 1864 these Acts were amended by raising the minimum sentence of penal servitude to five years, and providing that no sentence of penal servitude of less than seven years should be passed on second conviction, but this latter provision was repealed in 1879.

It has been seen that from the earliest times a sentence of transportation has never involved confinement in prison for the whole period. A large proportion of persons so sentenced, including all seven years' convicts, were retained in the hulks and never sent to the colonies, and these were generally released with free pardons when from half to three-fourths of their sentences had expired. The rules made in 1853 and 1857 reduced this irregular custom to a ticket-of-leave system, and when an increase of crime, marked by an outbreak of a practice of garroting, occurred about 1863, the public without reason attributed it to this system. It was probably with more reason attributed to the discharge within a short period of the flood of criminals who had been pent up during the change of system; but the Royal Commission in that year recommended, beside the changes embodied in the Act of 1864, a more complete and stringent control over the offender while on ticket-of-leave.

The foregoing sketch of the steps by which we have arrived at our present convict system will enable the following details of it to be understood. They are intended to combine the principles of deterring from the commission of crime and reforming the offender.

A sentence of penal servitude is, in its main features, and so far as concerns the punishment, applied on exactly the same system to every person subjected to it. The previous career and character of the prisoner makes no difference in the punishment to which he is subjected, because it is rightly considered that it is for the Courts of Law, who have, or should have, a full knowledge on these points, to consider them in awarding the sentence; and if any prisoner were subjected to harsher or milder treatment in consequence of any knowledge the prison authorities might have of his previous character, it might be that he would practically be punished twice over on the same account, and on information much less complete than the Court of Law would have at its command. The Government would also always be liable to charges of showing favour to or prejudice against certain particular prisoners; and any feeling of this kind would be fraught with danger and inconvenience.

It is also considered, and justly, that the Judge or Court who passes the sentence should know, or should be able to know, the exact effect of the sentence, and this would be impossible if any discretion rested with the executive officers as to the mode of carrying out the punishments.

A sentence of penal servitude is divided into three principal stages. During the first stage, which endures for nine months in all cases, the prisoner passes his whole time—excepting the period allotted to prayers and exercise—in his cell, apart from all other prisoners, working at some employment of an industrial or remunerative character. During the second he sleeps and has his meals in a separate cell, but works in association under a close and strict supervision, at employment suited to him. The third period is that during which he is conditionally released from prison, but kept under the supervision of the police, and liable, for any infraction of the conditions of his release, to be returned to prison, there to fulfil the portion of his sentence which remained unexpired at the time of his release. A stage, intermediate between the public works and the conditional release, is applied to women, who may be sent for nine months before their release on license to "refuges,"—establishments managed by private persons, who interest themselves in preparing the women for discharge, and in procuring suitable situations for them.

It is not possible here to state in detail the rules laid down for the treatment of prisoners in the three stages, but an outline of the objects which are aimed at may be given.

The first stage is one of severe penal discipline, during which the prisoner's mind is thrown in upon itself, and the prisoner cannot fail to feel that, however agreeable may have been his previous life, probably one of idleness and excitement, he pays dearly for it by the dull monotony, hard work, a diet which is sufficient, but no more than sufficient, and deprivation of every luxury he has been accustomed to indulge in; and, above all, by the absence of freedom, and the constant supervision which is his present condition, and which form his prospects for some years to come.

During this time he becomes open to lessons of admonition and warning; religious influences have full opportunity of obtaining access to him; he is put in that condition when he is likely to feel sorrow for the past and to welcome the words of those who show him how to avoid evil for the future.

I have said that this stage of a prisoner's sentence endures for nine months, and it may naturally occur to any one to ask, if its effects are both penal and reformatory, such as I have described and believe them to be, why the same treatment should not be followed throughout the whole of the sentence? The reason is, that it has always been held that we must bear in mind that the prisoner should not only be punished and *taught* what is right, but should be returned to society fitted both morally and physically to fulfil his proper duties in the battle of life.

It cannot be expected that this object would be fulfilled by his perpetual seclusion in a cell for years, with no communication with his fellows, an artificial state of existence absolutely opposed to that which nature points out as the condition of mental, moral, and physical health, and entirely unlike that which he is to be prepared to follow on his discharge from prison.

When the system of separate confinement was first established in the model prison at Pentonville, in 1842, the duration of the period of separate confinement was fixed at eighteen months. It was carried out with considerable rigour, and results showed themselves which could not be neglected. It was shown incontestably, as the Reports of the Commissioners demonstrated, that the minds of the prisoners became enfeebled by long-continued isolation; and, after various trials, the present term of nine months was fixed on as the longest to which prisoners could, with advantage, be subjected to this stage of the discipline. No doubt a modified system of separate confinement suitable to longer periods might be introduced, and it would then be possible to legalise sentences between the two years which is the maximum sentence of "imprisonment," and the five years which is the minimum sentence of "penal servitude"; and this course, which was recommended by the Lords' Committee of 1864, would be easy now that the prison system throughout the country has been made uniform by being placed under the Government.

The distinction made by the use of the term "imprisonment," to denote sentences of two years and under, and "penal servitude," to denote sentences of five years and upwards, no longer has any significance, now that they are both carried out in the United Kingdom, and it is misleading, for both classes of prisoners are undergoing "imprisonment," and are equally in a condition of "penal servitude." The only point to be kept in view is that the treatment should be adapted to the length of the sentence.

The use of the term "hard labour," in imposing the sentence of imprisonment, which is not used in passing one of penal servitude, might also well be omitted, for any prisoner sentenced to imprisonment should be, and is by law, required to labour, under specified conditions, suitable to his health and his capacity; and, in fact, excepting the specific kind of labour called "First Class Hard Labour," defined in the "Prison Act, 1865," as "crank, tread-wheel, etc., and other like kind of labour," the term "hard" has no particular meaning, and its employment in the sentence makes no practical difference.

Keeping in view the principle that during his imprisonment the convict is to be prepared and enabled to lead a reformed life when he is discharged, attention is paid, more especially during the first period, both to his moral, mental, and literary education.

Every prison has its staff of ministers of religion,

who, in prisons which contain large numbers, are not permitted to have any other duties, and who, therefore, can devote their whole time to the improvement and advantage of the prisoners placed under their spiritual care.

The advantage of thus inculcating religious feelings will not be contested by any one; and, notwithstanding the doubts which have arisen from injudicious exaggerations of the results of these influences, and by misconception of the true position of and functions fulfilled by the chaplains of prisons, it is certain that these advantages are much appreciated by prisoners, and that the exertions of the ministers of religion bear perhaps as much fruit as in the world outside.

The prison library and educational departments are in charge of the chaplain. Books are supplied to the prisoners, both of a purely religious and of an instructive character; and those who are uneducated are taught by a staff of schoolmasters at least the elements of reading and writing; those who have already some knowledge have opportunities and encouragement to improve themselves. As a knowledge of reading and writing affords so much opportunity for mental and moral improvement, and may have so important an effect on a prisoner's well-being in after life, inducements are offered to prisoners to exert themselves to attain it, by rendering some of the subsequent privileges a prisoner may gain conditional on his being able to read and write. For example, no convict can be promoted to the first class unless he can read and write; and after he has been under instruction a sufficient time, he is obliged, if he wishes to enjoy the privilege of communicating by letter with his friends, to do it himself, and without assistance. Of course, exceptions to these rules are made in the cases of men who, from age or mental incapacity, cannot be expected to acquire even the elements of knowledge.

Half-yearly examinations are held, to show the progress each prisoner makes, the result of which may be seen in the Yearly Reports of the Directors of Convict Prisons, and it is found that many prisoners who had not been able either to read or write when convicted, had learned to do both while in prison; and most of the remainder had made advances in the knowledge which they previously possessed.

After passing the allotted time in this stage, the convict is removed to a prison where he is employed at labour in restricted association, generally labour on public works, or farming, clearing or reclaiming land, and so on; but as there are some men who are not adapted for this kind of employment, bootmaking, tailoring, and other indoor employments are also carried on.

In whatever stage of his sentence a convict may be, he is always provided with a separate cell which he occupies at all times when not at work, at prayers, or at exercise. The sick or invalids are necessarily more associated, but as the infirmaries recently constructed place the great majority in separation, the chances of contamination therein are reduced to a minimum.

Great pains are taken, however, during the stage of a sentence of penal servitude in which prisoners labour in association, to prevent evil effect from contamination, by the hardened offenders, of those less versed in crime.

With this object, arrangements were adopted, in 1877-78, for separating the worst criminals from the rest; and moreover, as it was considered that the conversation which passed between prisoners during the times of exercise was a great medium of evil communication, steps were taken to prevent this bad effect. There is every reason to believe that these measures have had good results.

In 1879-80, another important measure was adopted, with the same object, viz. the formation of a class in which prisoners not versed in crime should be collected, so that their contamination by old offenders might be impossible.

Searching inquiries are made in order to ensure proper selection of prisoners for this class; for it is of the greatest consequence to prevent corrupt and cunning criminals who have evaded convictions, though they have deserved it, from gaining admission into this class and leading the well-disposed among them astray.

The reports which have been received of the good conduct and industry of these prisoners give reason to hope that this measure will be entirely successful.

Every convict may, during his sentence, pass through four classes, called the probation, the third, the second, and the first class, and certain selected prisoners are also placed, during the last year of their sentences, in a special class.

The probation class must last for one year; nine months of it are passed in a close prison, as already stated, the other three months on public works.

The third and second classes must each last for one year at least, and the remainder of the sentence may be passed in the first class, unless a prisoner is promoted to the special class, into which he may enter during his last year.

Promotion into each of these classes is followed by certain privileges, and each class wears its own distinctive badge.

These privileges are necessarily very limited, but still they offer inducements which are much sought after.

All privileges of increased diet have been abolished since 1864, as it was justly thought that to hold out prospects of food as an inducement to good behaviour was to appeal to the baser feelings, such as a good moral education should endeavour to suppress; and, secondly, because it was found that unfavourable impressions were produced outside by comparing the diet of the prisoner who enjoyed these slight improvements in the quantity or quality of the food with that of the honest hard-working free man, whose scanty means were hardly sufficient to keep himself and family in health.

The diet, in fact, is fixed at the minimum necessary to enable a man to execute the work required of him, but if he should be idle and not execute the work, then the amount of his food is reduced.

The advantages offered, therefore, by the higher classes, consist in the more frequent communications by visit or letter with their friends, in more freedom for exercise on Sundays, and in the earning of a higher gratuity of money to be paid on the prisoner's discharge.

The period which a prisoner passes in each class is measured, not simply by time, but by days of hard work, on the system of marks.

In addition to the immediate privileges which a

prisoner can gain by promotion to a higher class, he is offered the still greater, though more distant advantage, of slightly diminishing the duration of his sentence by obtaining "Conditional Release."

The amount of remission which any prisoner may gain is one-fourth of the whole period he passes on public works, and this remission is gained by industry alone, and not by "good conduct," which, in a prison, can be little more than passive, or abstaining from acts of indiscipline or irregularity. The time has long gone by, if ever it existed, when he could profit by any lip professions of piety or reformation.

On the other hand, acts of misconduct may be followed by forfeiture of remission, degradation to a lower class, and the consequent loss of privileges gained by industry, as well as by close confinement, reduction in diet, corporal punishment, and so on, and if, by repeated misbehaviour, a prisoner shows that his treatment in the close prison has not had its due effect upon him, and that he is not fit for associated employment on public works, he may be ordered to undergo the discipline of second probation for such period as may be thought necessary; or if during the course of his whole sentence he conducts himself badly, he may be ordered to pass the last six months in separate confinement, so that the deterrent effect of that discipline may be impressed on his mind when he is set free.

The power of punishing a prisoner is vested only in the Governor and in the Director.

The limits of punishment in both cases are laid down by the Secretary of State, and no punishment can be awarded without full investigation of the charge, conducted in the presence of the prisoner. The Governor has powers sufficient to deal with minor offences, and every punishment he orders is reported to the Director with a statement of the prisoner's offence.

The Director, whose functions are by statute those of a Visiting Justice, awards punishments for offences of a graver character. Only the Director has power to award corporal punishment, and he only for certain offences defined by the Secretary of State, and after full inquiry on oath conducted in the most formal manner. No unusual punishments may be inflicted.

Chains, handcuffs, or means of special restraint may not be made use of except under certain defined circumstances, and under strict regulations, and the use of them is always reported and recorded in a formal manner.

It can hardly be necessary to add that no officer is allowed to strike or abuse a prisoner. Should he find it necessary, on account of the violence of any prisoner, to make use of his weapons, he is always called upon to show that he confined himself strictly to the necessities of the occasion, or failing to do so he must bear the consequences.

The effect of the system of rewards and punishments, by which order and discipline are maintained in the prisons, is shown by the following statement of the number of prisoners punished. During the year 1871, of 13,582 males who were in the prisons, 6796 did not break the rules in any way, and 6347 were actually punished. Of 2184 females who were during the year in the prisons, 1414 did not break the rules, and 689 were actually punished.

Fourteen years latter—1884-85—with 13,619 male

prisoners in the prisons, 8639 did not commit any breach of the rules, and 4980 only were actually punished. Similarly, with 1265 females, 936 kept free of punishment, only 329 being punished. The comparison of these figures shows very satisfactory advance in good conduct among the prisoners; for, in the latter, the number not infringing the rules was greater by 1843, and the actual number punished was less by 1367; and, in the case of the females, the proportion who were free of offence was also larger.

The return of prison offences also proves that the great bulk of them are committed by a small number of habitual offenders against the rules.

Out of 27,835 prisoners discharged from convict prisons between 1871 and 1885, only about 1898 failed to earn some remission from their sentences. Many had never misconducted themselves at all, and a large proportion had gone through their imprisonment of many years with only some trifling breach of regulations recorded against them.

These facts are very significant. The result is not due to an easy and slack system, under which offences are passed over without report and without punishment; on the contrary, it will be apparent, even to a casual visitor, and is well known to those who are more intimately acquainted with the interior of the prisons, that order is strictly maintained in them, and that the discipline is exact without being severe.

It is evident, in fact, that in this respect, at all events, our system produces the result it is intended to do, but more especially it shows that the organisation of the department is effective, and that the staff of officers perform their duties with resolution and with judgment.

In order to maintain a strict and exact discipline, without exciting constant resistance, it is above all things necessary that the prisoners should feel that the rules are carried out justly and fairly, that the officers are simply administering the law, and that in case of any abuse of power on the part of an officer, he will be held answerable for it.

To this end every prisoner has unrestricted right of appeal against the act of those above him; he may lay his complaint in the first instance before the Governor, who is bound to investigate it, and to place the appeal on record, or he may appeal, either by written or personal application, to the higher authority of the Director, who can, if he sees fit, reverse or modify the decision of the Governor. The Director not coming in daily contact with the officers and prisoners, but only visiting the prison magisterially at uncertain intervals, it is, of course, felt that he can give a fresh and an impartial consideration to any question or complaint.

Besides this, the prisoners have the power of petitioning the Secretary of State.

Prisoners may also appeal to the independent visitors, who can, at any time they consider expedient, visit the prisons and inquire into the state of the prisoners and the discipline and condition of the prisons; but they have no power to give any order, or to interfere in any way with the administration of the prison.

As a matter of fact, prisoners exercise freely all these rights of appeal and petition.

The effect of these provisions is, not only that

prisoners feel that they cannot be unfairly dealt with, but the officers are constantly reminded that they are liable to have to answer for any abuse of their power.

The plan by which we endeavour to bring before the prisoner, in a form easily intelligible to him, that, as in ordinary life, the advantages held out to him as an encouragement to industry are directly proportioned to his industry; that he cannot be idle for a day without a corresponding loss; that good conduct is necessary as well as industry, because ill conduct will deprive him of the advantages he would gain by his industry;—is effected by a system of recording the industry by marks. It is not possible to set out the details of the system, but the principle on which it is framed, and an outline of the mode of carrying it out may be given.

To every convict is assigned the duty of earning a number of marks proportioned to the length of his sentence. These marks are awarded to each prisoner according to the degree of his industry: if the prisoner earns them at the lowest rate he will serve out the whole of his sentence; should he earn the highest rate, he will get off about one-fourth; if at any intermediate rate, he then will earn proportionate remission.

The record by marks applies not only to the amount of remission the prisoner can gain from his sentence, but also to every step in the classes he passes through during his imprisonment; for instance, he is required to pass at least a year in each of the classes, but during that time he must earn a definite number of marks, or else his promotion is delayed; and, further, the gratuity which he earns in each class is calculated according to the number of marks he earns.

To ensure a fair value in marks being assigned to each man's industry, not only is a rigid supervision and check maintained on the working parties by the principal warders, the chief warder, deputy governor, and governor, who pay particular and especial attention to this point; but the prisoners' work is measured by a staff of professional officers, employed for the purpose, who act quite independently of the regular discipline staff, and whose measurements are priced out in money, and afford a check and test of the correctness of the assignment of the marks of industry.

Every prisoner is furnished with a card, on which, periodically, his earnings in marks are recorded, and, if he feels himself unfairly dealt with, he has free right to complain, and his grievances are investigated.

In this manner, day by day, week by week, and year by year, he can count and record the progress he is making towards an advance in class, in accumulation of money, and towards conditional release; and he is made perfectly to see and feel that his fate is in his own hands, and that he has something more to work and to hope for than the mere avoidance of punishment.

The course followed with regard to the female convicts is in the main the same as described with more particular reference to the men. They may earn, however, a larger proportion of remission, viz. one-third of their whole sentences; and to those whose good conduct and character justifies the hope of complete amendment, a further advantage is held out by their being allowed to pass the nine months immediately preceding the term of their release in the "refuges" established and managed by private effort, assisted by contributions from the Government, which have been already referred to. These "refuges" are not prisons either in appearance or in discipline—they are *homes*, and are intended to afford the advantages of a treatment approaching in its characteristics to that of home influence.

This being a general view of the course a prisoner goes through in fulfilling a sentence of penal servitude, some slight detail may be given of the manner in which some parts of it are carried out.

It has for many years been an established principle in English convict prisons to endeavour to instil into the convicts habits of industry, to develop their intelligence by employing them on industrial labour, and to facilitate their entering the ranks of honest industry on their discharge, by giving them facilities for acquiring a knowledge of trades. These objects are fortunately conducive to another very desirable result, viz. that of making the prisons self-supporting in various degrees.

The employment of prisoners may be made to conduce to any or all of three objects—firstly, to create a deterrent effect on the prisoner himself and on the criminal class; secondly, to produce a reformatory effect on the prisoner himself; and, thirdly, to recoup, as far as possible, the cost of maintaining the prison.

The following remarks, made by Lord Carnarvon in his address to the Prison Congress of 1872, indicate clearly the relative importance of these objects:—

But there is a school which holds—and I believe the opinion to be as dangerous as it is attractive—that all prison labour ought to be remunerative, and that the great, if not the primary object of a prison is to make it self-supporting. But, as was stated by the House of Lords' Committee in 1863, whatever may be the actual incomings from prison work, "a profitable return from industrial employment ought not to be made the test of prison efficiency." If, indeed, it were so considered, it must lead to a relaxed discipline, and an injurious influence on the mind of the prisoner. Where, indeed, the sentence is of sufficient length, it may have the happiest effects upon the offender; but it ought to follow upon the harder and more penal labour, and ought not to be made the equivalent for it. Whilst on this subject, I will only add that the actual profits of industrial work must necessarily vary with the circumstances of different prisons. The use of machinery, the state of the neighbouring markets, the class of prisoners, the particular employments, the number of men available, and the consequent power of sub-dividing them for the purposes of work, are all-important conditions; and in proportion as they are wanting, the less productive and profitable will the returns be.

The attempt to make prison labour profitable is subject to certain considerable impediments, arising from the individual peculiarities of the prisoner class, the absence of the ordinary stimulus which operates on men in a state of freedom, and the inconvenience and prejudice against Government trading.

A large number of prisoners are persons who are absolutely unable, or find it extremely difficult, through mental or physical incapacity, to earn their livelihood, even under favourable circumstances. The result of a medical census of the convict prisons on 4th April 1881, giving an analysis of the mental and physical condition of the convict prison population, was to show that a large proportion of prisoners, on account of these conditions, would be, even if out of prison, in a greater or less degree a charge on the public. It is hopeless, therefore, to expect them to repay by their labour any considerable portion of the cost of their custody and maintenance in prison.

Prison labour, moreover, must always be carried on

under the disadvantage that the worker is without the stimulus afforded by the prospect of *immediate* resulting benefit. He is, of necessity, housed, clothed, and fed, and modern feelings of humanity have, in fact, led to his being in these matters placed in a better position than many who have not forfeited their liberty, and who are dependent for the daily supply of their necessities on their daily exertions.

In some foreign countries, where great importance is attached to the object of making the prisons pay, the prisoners are allowed to draw and to expend a certain portion of their earnings on various small luxuries, such as additional and better food, tobacco, etc.; a certain other portion is set aside for them on their discharge, and the Government takes the remainder. In convict prisons in England a prisoner was at one time allowed to profit, more or less immediately and directly, by his industry, by obtaining more or better food in prison, and a larger sum of money on discharge. This gave rise to a great deal of hostile criticism. It was said that prisoners might enjoy luxuries, such as food which many an honest poor man had to deny himself, and that this, with the fact of his being on discharge, in possession of a sum of money which an honest hard-working labourer would be unable to accumulate, led to a comparison favourable to a dishonest instead of an honest career. Public opinion, therefore, demanded that prisoners throughout their sentence should have only the barest necessaries in the way of food, and just sufficient money on discharge to enable them to maintain themselves while seeking employment, purchasing tools, etc.; and this sound principle was adopted by a

Royal Commission which, in 1863, inquired into the subject of prison management, and has been carried out.

The only stimulus, therefore, which can be offered to a prisoner is that of gaining by his industry a remission of some portion of his sentence, of improving his prison class, or that of punishing him if he is idle. Even with these means, however, by steady supervision, very good results are obtained. But there are prisoners, chiefly the habitual criminal, who sometimes prefer any punishment which involves a partial relief from labour to the steady industry required on the public works.

The Government is always subject to a great deal of pressure in opposition to its undertaking to manufacture for itself, and still more if it manufactures for the market; and when these manufactures are carried on by prison labour, a certain specious objection is made on the ground of their thereby competing with free labour, and lowering the wages of free workmen. Of course this is utterly unreasonable; but, nevertheless, it has a considerable effect. The particular trade which happens to suffer from the competition of prison labour is naturally loud in its outcries, and can always find active advocates; and, on the principle that everybody's business is nobody's business, this agitation is not counterbalanced by a corresponding agitation on behalf of the public, and in aid of those who act in the public interest. The customs of trade societies are also adverse to the action of Government in this way.

It is so obvious as hardly to require stating, that, as persons who are earning a livelihood while free are competing with somebody or other, so it is perfectly reasonable that they should work, and therefore compete equally after being put in prison. I doubt whether such employment should be carried on in prisons as requires the purchase, from public funds, of a large and expensive plant and machinery, the value of work done by which would bear a great proportion to the value of the prisoners' labour, because in such a case it is not merely competition against prison labour, but against Government capital. Many of the disadvantages which attend the system of making prisons into manufactories are avoided by performing in them work required by the Government, either central or local; and certainly work of this kind should be preferred to any other.

The most practical way of achieving the three objects to be attained by the industrial employment of prisoners —viz., to deter them by its penal character; to reform them by its operation on their moral feelings; and to contribute towards the expenses of their maintenance, —is to divide the period of punishment into different stages, during one of which the penal or deterrent object should be principally considered: during the other, the reformatory and pecuniary may prevail in various degrees.

The most effective continuous punishment (besides loss of liberty) which can be inflicted on a prisoner consists of strict isolation from the social enjoyment and companionship of his fellows, diet reduced to the barest necessaries, deprivation of all the comforts and luxuries which men of the prisoner class usually allow themselves, such as tobacco, drink, etc.; and among these I may mention the comfort to many among them of being slovenly, for many of those who visit our prisons remark on the cells as being so "clean and comfortable," whereas many prisoners, if they expressed their ideas on the subject, would call them "clean and uncomfortable."

In addition to these is the punishment of hard, dull, useless, uninteresting, monotonous labour. It is necessary to resort to this for its penal effect. There is, nevertheless, a limit to the time during which a prisoner can be advantageously subjected to it, for it is decidedly brutalising in its effects. To men of any intelligence it is irritating, depressing, and debasing to the mental faculties; to those already of a low type of intelligence, it is too conformable to the state of mind out of which it is most desirable that they should be raised.

Labour on cranks, etc., being a purely penal employment, is not carried on in convict prisons as part of the ordinary course, but if a prisoner persistently misconducts himself he may, if it is considered suitable to his case, be, for a limited time, employed at turning a crank.

If a prisoner has any knowledge of a trade which can be followed in prison, he is, if circumstances permit, assigned to such labour, for then the public profits, while the prisoner preserves his skill, and those prisoners who show an aptitude and a desire are selected, when opportunities offer, to learn any trade which is followed in the prison. It is obvious that the number of trades which can be followed in prison is very limited, and if possible the work should be such as cannot be equally well performed by machinery. Prison labour now supplies everything that can possibly be made by it for the prison service, such as clothing of all descriptions, bedding, cell furniture, cooperage, officers' uniforms, baskets, printing, bookbinding, cooking, baking, washing, etc. The manufacture of hammocks, seamen's bags, boarding bags, ships' fenders, coal sacks and bags, signal cones, baskets, hand hones, mail bags, stamping pads, labels, twine, boots, uniforms, knitted articles, hearth-rugs, mats and matting, tinware, anchor ranges, and register stoves, is carried on for other Government departments.

The following are some of the employments carried on in those convict prisons in which the prisoners are kept in isolation for a period of nine months, and the average daily value of their labour, ascertained by measuring their work and assigning trade prices to it:—

| | Average earnings per day. | | | | |
|---|---|---|---|---|---|
| | *s.* | *d.* | | *s.* | *d.* |
| Tailoring | 1 | 4 | to | 2 | 9 |
| Shoemaking | 1 | 3 | ,, | 1 | 11 |
| Matmaking | 0 | 7 | ,, | 0 | 10 |
| Weaving | 0 | 10 | ,, | 1 | 0 |
| Knitting | 0 | 3 | ,, | 0 | 5 |
| Oakum-picking | 0 | 0¼ | ,, | 0 | 0¾ |
| Needlework | 0 | 5 | ,, | 0 | 8 |
| Basketmaking | 1 | 2 | ,, | 1 | 4 |

Though it cannot be claimed that the problem of finding remunerative labour for prisoners in this stage has been fully solved, yet some progress has been made towards finding employment which plays its part as a moral reformatory agent on those who unfortunately are subject to prison discipline.

In the "public works" prisons, where they work in regulated association, the conditions of the work more resemble those which prevail outside, and it is obvious there is more chance of finding suitable work, and of its being such as may be useful to them on the conclusion of the sentences, of their being taught useful trades, and of the work being made to pay. Outdoor employment is considered best for most of the prisoners in this stage; it is healthiest both for body and mind, and it is the more appropriate to the circumstances, as generally it requires less skill.

Some years ago the convicts in England were employed in jobbing work about the dockyards; they worked in chains, scattered in gangs over the yard, and a great deal of the work was mere brute labour, such as dragging heavy loads, which would have been done far better and cheaper by horses. Such work and under such conditions is neither reformatory nor remunerative. Great improvements have since then been made in our system.

The system inaugurated at Portland, of executing large public works by means of prisoners' labour, is the best that has yet been devised. The Royal Commission, 1879, on the "Penal Servitude Acts," make the following observations and recommendations:—

> We are convinced also that severe labour on public works is most beneficial in teaching criminals habits of industry, and training them to such employments as digging, road-making, quarrying, stone-dressing, building, and brickmaking,—work of a kind which cannot be carried on in separate confinement. It is found that employment of this nature is most easily obtained by convicts on their release, since men are taken on for rough work without the strict inquiries as to previous character which are made in other cases.
>
> By far the most important work done by the convicts is that performed at the public works prisons. The magnificent breakwater and the fortifications at Portland, the great basins at Chatham

and Portsmouth, and other similar works, which have been mainly executed by convict labour, testify to the skill with which the system of associated labour has been directed, and are substantial proofs that convicts can be made to repay to the public a considerable part of the cost of their maintenance.

No doubt, even if it were not advantageous in a pecuniary point of view to employ convicts on public works of this nature, it would still be most desirable that such employment should be found for them as an essential part of penal discipline; but it is far more satisfactory that their labour should, if possible, be profitably employed.

The advantages of acquiring or practising a trade which is so highly appreciated by the prisoners, constitute a means of rewarding those who show themselves worthy of it. The moral effect of such employment is, as has been already stated, greater, and therefore more likely to make the prisoners fall into habits of useful industry than if they were always employed at work which must present itself in the most repulsive form to their minds; and important works may sometimes be executed by this means, which the public might not be always willing otherwise to undertake, though all can understand the advantages the nation may derive from a judicious utilisation of the labours of men who, whether usefully or uselessly employed, have to be maintained at the public expense.

The importance of the public works executed by convicts since the system was introduced is exemplified at Portland, where this labour has been employed in quarrying the stone for the construction of the breakwater—a stone dam in the sea, nearly two miles in length, and running into water 50 or 60 feet deep. They have also executed the barracks and the principal part of the works of defence, batteries, casemates, etc., on the island, which may be considered impregnable to any mode of attack except blockade and starvation of the garrison.

In executing these works, every variety of mechanics' work necessary in building or engineering has been executed by convicts—quarrying and dressing and placing the stone, all sorts of carpentry, casting and forging ironwork, and so on. The large and extensive plant has also been made and kept in repair by the convicts, including the construction of the large cranes and derricks in the quarries, and the laying of the rails for the quarry waggons to run upon on their way to the place for delivery of the stone.

The extensive works which have been undertaken of late years at Chatham and Portsmouth, for the enlargement of these dockyards, have been largely carried out by convict labour. At Chatham, the addition to the dockyard covers a space of 430 acres, which is four times the extent of the old dockyard. It occupies the site of St. Mary's Island, the channel which separated the island from the mainland furnishing the position of the three basins—viz., the "Repairing Basin," 21 acres; the "Factory Basin," 20 acres; the "Fitting-out Basin," 28 acres. The bottom of the basins is 12 feet below the old river-bed, and 32 feet below St. Mary's Island. The latter—which was formerly much intersected by creeks, and nearly covered at high water—has been raised about 8 feet by tipping and spreading on it the earth excavated out of the basins, etc. The whole island has been drained, and surrounded by a sea-wall and embankment 9200 feet, or nearly two miles in length, principally executed by convict labour.

In carrying out these works, the prisoners have been employed in excavating, pile-driving, and concreting, for the foundations ; bricklaying, concreting, stone-dressing, and setting, in connection with the construction of the basin walls and entrances; removing the earth from the area of the basin by means of waggons and incline planes, barrow roads, barrow lifts, and tipping waggons; loading and unloading materials; plate-laying; and attending standing and locomotive engines.

The basin walls (which show a height of 39 feet from the bottom of basin to the coping) have a height of 50 feet altogether, from the foundation gravel or chalk.

At Portsmouth similar operations have been performed by prisoners in making the large extensions of that dockyard, besides a vast quantity of preliminary work, such as demolishing the old fortifications.

The bricks used in these works have been made by convicts, to the number of 313,242,260, and the Portland stone required has been raised and worked by the convicts at Portland prison.

Work of a proportionally still higher pecuniary value has been done for the convict department, in the building of new prison accommodation, which has been rendered necessary on account of the prisoners who would have been transported having now to be retained in prisons in England; and for the improvement of prisons built on imperfect models. Since 1863 prison accommodation in cells for 4771 prisoners has been erected at convict prisons entirely by convict labour, with a number of accessory buildings, quarters for officers, and so on. The actual cost to the Government of buildings erected for the convict department, between 1863 and 1885, has been £358,700; the same work done by contract would have cost £636,400, showing a clear gain by convict labour of £277,700 in this comparatively small department of their labour. In these works the bricks were made, stone was quarried and dressed, timber sawn, and iron cast, forged, and wrought from the raw state by prisoners.

Among these works the largest are—a prison at Woking for 700 women, at Borstal for 500 men, and at Wormwood Scrubs for 1052 men. This latter was commenced by a party of 100 prisoners placed in a temporary prison inside a wooden hoarding. All the rest, including the making of the bricks, they have done themselves. They have added new wings to the prisons at Chatham (500 cells) and Portsmouth (200 cells); Dartmoor (272 cells), and an extension of two existing wings (318 cells); Parkhurst (535 cells), and Brixton (306 cells). At Pentonville an addition of 327 cells was made under rather peculiar circumstances. The ground space was so restricted that the only way to add to the prison was by raising the roof and adding a story; and this had to be done while the prisoners continued to inhabit the prison.

Although all the mechanics' work of these buildings is done by convicts, it must not be supposed that these mechanics are found ready to our hands among the prisoners. Out of 9107 prisoners in custody on 1st July 1882, 3914 were employed at trades, and 3235 or 82·6 per cent acquired their skill in the prison. Men thus employed will, it is hoped and believed, be less likely to relapse into crime on their discharge, as they will have full opportunities of pursuing an honest calling. Moreover, it is reported that the cases of misconduct are much fewer among those prisoners employed in trades than among those who are employed jobbing about, although the latter is much the easier work.

The following return shows the extent to which employment in trades is carried out in the convict prisons, and the variety of mechanics' work followed and taught:—

Number of convicts in prison, 1st July 1882—9107.

| TRADE. | Followed before Reception. | Learnt in Prison. | Total employed at Trades, etc. |
|---|---|---|---|
| Bagmakers . . . . | 1 | 17 | 18 |
| Bakers . . . . . | 18 | 51 | 69 |
| Basketmakers . . . | 3 | 41 | 44 |
| Bellhangers . . . . | ... | 2 | 2 |
| Blacksmiths . . . | 33 | 33 | 66 |
| Boilermakers . . . | 1 | ... | 1 |
| Bookbinders . . . | 5 | 29 | 34 |
| Bricklayers . . . | 45 | 187 | 232 |
| Brickmakers . . . | 1 | 2 | 3 |
| Carpenters . . . | 92 | 151 | 243 |
| Chairmakers . . . | 1 | ... | 1 |
| Chimney-sweeps . . | 2 | 8 | 10 |
| Cooks . . . . . | ... | 97 | 97 |
| Coopers . . . . | 3 | 3 | 6 |
| Coppersmiths . . . | ... | 1 | 1 |
| Engineers, mechanical . | 4 | ... | 4 |
| Engine Drivers . . . | 5 | 12 | 17 |
| Fitters, engine . . . | 7 | 4 | 11 |
| Fitters, gas, etc. . . | 12 | 16 | 28 |
| Fitters, iron, . . . | 3 | 2 | 5 |
| Fitters, ordinary . . | 12 | 13 | 25 |
| Flax Dressers . . . | 1 | 10 | 11 |
| Galvanisers . . . | ... | 1 | 1 |
| Carry forward . . | 249 | 680 | 929 |

| Trade. | Followed before Reception. | Learnt in Prison. | Total employed at Trades, etc. |
|---|---|---|---|
| Brought forward | 249 | 680 | 929 |
| Gardeners | 10 | 84 | 94 |
| Grinders | 3 | ... | 3 |
| Knitters | ... | 251 | 251 |
| Locksmiths | ... | 1 | 1 |
| Masons | 45 | 68 | 113 |
| Matmakers | ... | 51 | 51 |
| Moulders | 3 | ... | 3 |
| Moulders, brass | 1 | ... | 1 |
| Moulders, iron | 14 | 9 | 23 |
| Painters | 35 | 24 | 59 |
| Paperhangers | 1 | ... | 1 |
| Plasterers | 18 | 5 | 23 |
| Platelayers | 3 | 104 | 107 |
| Plumbers | 6 | 4 | 10 |
| Polishers, French | 2 | ... | 2 |
| Printers | 8 | 34 | 42 |
| Riggers | 2 | 13 | 15 |
| Sail or Hammockmakers | 2 | 67 | 69 |
| Sawyers, stone | ... | 91 | 91 |
| Sawyers, wood | 13 | 39 | 52 |
| Ships' fender makers | ... | 10 | 10 |
| Shoemakers | 85 | 482 | 567 |
| Slaters | 10 | 10 | 20 |
| Smiths | 2 | 1 | 3 |
| Stonecutters | 26 | 364 | 390 |
| Strikers | 15 | 59 | 74 |
| Tailors | 109 | 634 | 743 |
| Tailors' repairs | ... | 31 | 31 |
| Tinsmiths | 10 | 19 | 29 |
| Turners | 2 | 3 | 5 |
| Washers | ... | 7 | 7 |
| Weavers | 2 | 86 | 88 |
| Wheelwrights | 3 | 4 | 7 |
| Totals | 679 | 3235 | 3914 |

The department which manages the convict prisons is founded on statutes earlier than that which has been described as creating the Department of Local Prisons.

The Secretary of State for the Home Department is the supreme head of all prisons. All rules are issued under his authority and with his approval, and must, of course, be consistent with the Acts of Parliament.

The convict prisons are managed by the Chairman and Board of Directors of Convict Prisons, who were constituted by 13 & 14 Vict. cap. 39, and exercise all the powers formerly vested by Acts of Parliament in the various bodies who managed the prisons placed under their control. As already related, the first prison establishments in England, created specially to contain convicts under sentence of transportation prior to or in lieu of removal to the penal colonies, were the hulks, established as a temporary expedient in 1776; afterwards Millbank was opened in 1816, to which prisoners might be sent for imprisonment instead of being sentenced to transportation (34 Geo. III. cap. 84); and Pentonville was opened in 1842 (5 Vict. cap. 29). Special Acts of Parliament were passed from time to time to constitute these establishments, and provide for their administration and inspection.

The cost of maintaining the prisoners in the hulks was undertaken by the Government in 1779. These establishments were at first managed by local justices. Such supervision as there was over them in their early days was exercised by the Court of King's Bench. Gradually, however, the Home Office seems to have assumed a power of inspection and control, which was legalised in 1815, and their connection with the King's Bench was finally severed in 1825. The supervision was then vested in a paid superintendent (5 Geo. IV. cap. 84): this office was abolished in 1846 (9 & 10

Vict. cap. 26), and their management vested in "a person" until it was transferred to the Directors as above related.

The management of Millbank was, at first, placed in the hands of a special unpaid Committee, then paid Inspectors were appointed (6 & 7 Vict. cap. 26), and subsequently Visitors (11 & 12 Vict. cap. 104). Pentonville was, when first opened, supervised and controlled by a body of unpaid Commissioners (5 Vict. cap. 29).

The lists of the members of these Committees and Commissions contain the names of some of the most distinguished men and eminent statesmen of their day. It had not yet been discovered that collecting into a board of management a number of persons with high-sounding names was the least effective and the most irresponsible mode of administration that could be devised, and consequently while passing through these various phases, the management and discipline of prisoners formed the subject of many Committees of Inquiry and Acts of Parliament. As a final result, it was found desirable to substitute for these various disconnected unpaid bodies one paid body, who could devote their whole attention to their important duties, and thus originated the Board of Directors of Convict Prisons.

It is the duty of the Directors to visit every convict prison periodically. Every prison is inspected monthly —some weekly,—to see that the orders given are carried out, that there are no abuses or irregularities, to hear appeals or requests from prisoners, and to act magisterially in trying charges against prisoners. Independent visitors, hereafter referred to, inspect the convict prisons when they think proper, and hear any complaints prisoners may desire to prefer.

The whole of the financial affairs of the convict and local prisons, the making of contracts, and those administrative duties of conduct and discipline which require the intervention of higher authority than the Governors in immediate charge of the prisons, are performed for the convict prisons by the Directors, and for the local prisons by the Commissioners.

The necessary funds are voted every year by Parliament, the Directors and Commissioners being respectively responsible for their administration according to instructions received.

Although the various prison departments are constituted under different Acts of Parliament, they are practically amalgamated into one, and in due course will no doubt be entirely. The offices of Surveyor-General of prisons, Chairman of the Directors of convict prisons, and Inspector-General of military prisons, and Chairman of Commissioners of prisons, are, and always have been, united in the same person. The Directors of convict prisons act also as Inspectors of military prisons.

Each prison has a governor, a chaplain, and a medical officer, and, where necessary, a deputy-governor, an assistant-chaplain, a Roman Catholic priest, and an assistant-medical officer.

The governor is the head of the establishment; under him are more immediately the discipline staff of warders, etc. The schoolmasters, while more immediately under the chaplain, and the infirmary staff under the medical officer, are nevertheless subject to the governor in all matters of discipline.

There is also a clerk of works, or other officer of lower grade, and, according as they are required, permanent officers to instruct the prisoners in their various trades, and to measure the value of the work they execute.

More minute details of the staff at any prison are to be found in the Annual Reports of the Directors of Convict Prisons, of the Prison Commissioners, and in the estimates laid before the House of Commons.

The detailed instructions to officers, under which the prisons are administered, will be found in the rules for prisons. It must suffice here to say that the spirit of these instructions is, that while it is always to be remembered that the prisoners are sentenced to undergo punishment, the dictates of humanity are to be carefully kept in view; that all the officers are to bear in mind that their duty is to reform as well as to punish, and that the conditions to ensure good health of body are to be carefully attended to. These instructions are by no means allowed to be neglected, and statistics prove the efficiency of the organisation for this purpose.

From the time when the English Government took seriously in hand the reform of the prison system, nearly forty years ago, their efforts have been directed to forming a good staff of officers as a matter of the first consequence, and these appointments have never been considered the subject of political patronage or private interest. This feature might indeed be considered one of the leading characteristics of the English prison system, and to which it owes in a great measure its success. In introducing it—at a time when it was considered quite the right and natural thing for a Minister to use public appointments to provide berths for his friends and for their friends, and in enforcing it during all his tenure of office—Sir George Grey conferred a lasting benefit on the country, and gave a striking proof of his high mind and public spirit.

Appointments and promotions in the prisons are made by authority of the Secretary of State, on the recommendation of the Department of Prisons, except in certain cases, in which, either by law or by the authority of the Secretary of State, the appointments and promotions are made without referring each individual case to him.

The conditions required of all candidates for appointment are that they shall be suitable as to character, physique, and intelligence.

Those applicants are preferred who have already filled with credit situations in which similar qualifications are requisite. Confidential inquiries are made from those who are able and competent to give the necessary information as to the manner in which a candidate has performed those duties, and on his general character and disposition in the various points which are of most importance for the position he seeks to fill.

A large number of applications for the appointments are from men who have left the army, because from the nature of the engagements under which men enter the army, there is always a flow of candidates for such employment as prison and other Government service offers, but there is no rule restricting the choice of officers of prisons to them. Their habits of order and discipline, of rendering and enforcing strict obedience, and their aptitude in dealing with large bodies of men, are unquestionably very valuable qualities for the office, and if not possessed by an officer on joining, would have to be acquired more or less perfectly afterwards.

All candidates who are nominated to posts in the prison service are obliged, like all other civil servants, to obtain a certificate of qualification from the Civil Service Commissioners, that they fulfil the conditions laid down for each appointment, in respect to character, education, age, etc.

Subordinate (discipline) officers all enter either as assistant warders or civil guards, and having obtained certificates of the Civil Service Commissioners, are appointed on a probation of three months; if, during that period, they do not show any aptitude for the service, they are discharged with a week's notice.

Officers in the prison service are not entitled to any advantages or allowances besides their regular pay and allowances; they are not allowed to make use of, or derive any benefit from, the labour of the prisoners.

The punishments to which officers are subjected consist of fines, degradation to a lower rank, or dismissal. Certain special offences are also punishable by imprisonment, after conviction before a proper court—viz., aiding or attempting to aid a prisoner to escape, and bringing into the prison, or taking out, for prisoners, articles not allowed by the rules.

It may be well to give a short *résumé* of the principles which our experience might be said to have established. They are—(1.) That a well-devised system of secondary punishment should provide for subjecting those sentenced to it to a uniform course of penal deterrent discipline. (2.) That every means possible should be adopted for developing and working on the higher feelings of the prisoners, directly by moral, religious, and secular instruction, and indirectly by ensuring industry, good conduct, and discipline, through appealing to the hope of advantage or reward, as well as by the fear of punishment. (3.) That, with a view to deterrence as well as reformation, it is desirable that every short sentence and the first part of every long sentence should be undergone on the separate system as developed at Pentonville. (4.) That before discharging the long-sentenced convict to a full or modified degree of liberty, he should be subjected to further training, in which he should be associated, under supervision, while at labour, but separated at all other times. (5.) That properly constructed prison buildings, providing among other things for this separation, are all-important requisities for the success of the system. (6.) That employment should be provided and industry enforced or encouraged for all. (7.) That care should be taken to select and train a good staff of skilled and responsible officials to supervise and carry on the work of the convict establishments, and means adopted to prevent their work being hindered or defeated by the prisoners being brought into close contact on works or otherwise with free men who were under no such responsibilities. (8.) That those who on discharge are disposed to follow honest courses should be guided and assisted in their endeavours, and that a careful watch should be kept over all till they have re-established their character.

The following figures show in a concise and striking form the effects of this part of our penal system by the remarkable diminution in the number of persons detained under punishment for serious crime, and its progressive decrease as our system has developed in execution.

Total number of persons in custody under sentence of Penal Servitude and Transportation in England and the Colonies at the end of the following years :—

| | | | |
|---|---|---|---|
| Dec. 31, 1869 | 11,660. | Dec. 31, 1877 | 10,763. |
| ,, 1870 | 11,890. | ,, 1878 | 10,671. |
| ,, 1871 | 11,712. | Mar. 31, 1879 | 10,884. |
| ,, 1872 | 11,488. | ,, 1880 | 10,839. |
| ,, 1873 | 11,061. | ,, 1881 | 10,676. |
| ,, 1874 | 10,867. | ,, 1882 | 10,587. |
| ,, 1875 | 10,765. | ,, 1883 | 10,529. |
| ,, 1876 | 10,725. | ,, 1884 | 9,942. |
| | | ,, 1885 | 8,790. |

Taken together with the diminution in our local prison population, since those establishments were transferred to the Government in 1878 (see page 109), we had in 1885 no less than 5797 fewer prisoners in custody than at the corresponding period of the year in 1878, and there appears good prospect of this diminution being to a large extent permanent.

Taking the comparison back to the year before penal servitude was introduced, viz. 1852, it is shown in the Reports on Convict Prisons in that year that we were maintaining in Great Britain 8274 convicts, in Gibraltar and Bermuda 2650, in Van Diemen's Land 4762, and in West Australia 1450, or 17,130 in all, besides 5246 in Ireland. The convict population of Great Britain, therefore, was then about double what it is now, while the general population was only two-thirds; and this accumulation of convicts accrued in spite of the fact that those who were sentenced to seven years usually were discharged in this country at the end of three years, and might be at the end of two, and other sentences in like proportion, a life sentence involving no more than eleven and a half years or possibly only six.

The following table shows the remarkable decrease in the number of sentences of penal servitude during a term when the population has largely increased:—

| Average number of sentences of Penal Servitude in England and Wales. | | Average Population of England and Wales. |
|---|---|---|
| During 5 years ended 1859 | 2589. | 19,257,184. |
| ,, ,, 1864 | 2800. | 20,369,938. |
| ,, ,, 1869 | 1978. | 21,680,874. |
| ,, ,, 1874 | 1622. | 23,087,947. |
| ,, ,, 1879 | 1633. | 24,700,326. |
| During 5 years ended 1884 | 1428. | 26,213,629. |

During the last three years of this last period the numbers have averaged only 1367, showing a continual downward tendency.

These figures have a particular interest as showing that the number of sentences for serious crime have considerably diminished since transportation ceased to form part of our system, and might profitably be pondered by those countries which contemplate embarking in all the difficulties that system involves, under the idea that there is no other way out of their difficulties.

# CHAPTER VII.

## SUPERVISION—DISCHARGED PRISONERS' AID SOCIETIES.

It must not be assumed that when a prisoner is discharged from prison, having served his sentence or obtained a conditional release remitting some part of it, there is nothing more to be done. He may want a helping hand to put him in the right groove for earning an honest livelihood, and prevent him falling into the hands of those who would lead him astray; or he may need careful watching and reminding that he has got to regain his character before he can take his place in the community as a man whose crimes have been thoroughly and effectually purged.

The "Prevention of Crimes Act, 1871," affords the means of fulfilling the latter object. Under section 8 thereof any person convicted a second time on indictment may be sentenced to be subject to the supervision of the police for seven years or less after the expiration of his sentence, and during such period he is required to keep the police informed of his residence, and to report himself to them once a month, failing which he is liable to a year's imprisonment with hard labour. A prisoner released from a sentence of penal servitude on remission of a part of his sentence is subject to similar obligations and penalties; and further, if it is shown that there are reasonable grounds for believing that he is getting his livelihood by dishonest means, or in other ways shown that he is not worthy of the freedom conditionally conferred on him, he is liable to be returned to prison to undergo the portion of his sentence which was remitted. A person convicted on indictment after a previous conviction is also considered not to be entitled for seven years to the presumption of innocence under certain circumstances of suspicion, which is the right of every member of the community whose character is untainted.

It is obvious that to enable supervision to be effectually carried out, and to ensure, so far as possible, that an old offender should, on reconviction, be recognised as such, it is necessary to have a good and complete personal record of the members of the criminal classes, accessible to all police forces and courts of justice.

With this view the "Habitual Criminals Act, 1869," directed the formation of a central register of criminals. A very wide interpretation was at first given to this direction, and the number of persons registered accumulated so rapidly, when all cases were entered in it, that the register was becoming almost useless from its bulk, and it was, moreover, not generally so useful as desirable, as it was accessible only in London. In 1876, therefore, it was determined to confine the register to prisoners of the doubly-convicted class described in sections 7 and 8 of the "Prevention of Crimes Act, 1871," and arrangements were made for printing it.

The register is now therefore printed and circulated to all police forces and prisons all over the kingdom.

The printing is done by convict prisoners. The first volume, published in 1876, embraces the period from 11th December 1869 to 31st March 1876, and contains the names of 12,164 persons, with 21,194 convictions recorded against them, and the detailed personal description of each one of them. Similar volumes, in continuation, have been published annually.

By means of the annual volumes the police authorities have at their command, in a most convenient and useful form, all information necessary to establish a *primâ facie* identification of any person suspected of being an habitual criminal, and are thereby able at once to procure direct from the locality or the prison where he is known, any further information, evidence, means of identification, photographs, etc., required.

It is believed that a list of this character is the first attempt of its kind to furnish generally, to all police bodies and others, information, complete and readily accessible, respecting the class of prisoners against whom they are carrying on their operations.

In addition to the foregoing, there has been issued a "Distinctive Marks Register," by which the police, when in doubt of, or unable to ascertain the name of, a person in custody, are enabled to trace his antecedents, from the fact that, in a vast proportion of cases, the habitual criminal carries on his person marks which afford a certain clue to his identity.

These two books give, in the fullest manner, and by two entirely distinct means of identification, the particulars necessary to assist the police in their attempts to check the habitual criminal in his career.

It is worthy of note that supervision and registry of

criminals was one of the features of the transportation system, which, therefore, in this as in so much else, we have imitated and profited by and developed in our modern prison systems.

The duty and advantage of helping prisoners to find employment after expiating their offence in prison was soon recognised when it began to be understood that the community had some duty to, and some interest in, those who had fallen into crime, besides that of terrifying them or revenging itself on them. The first statute in which this principle was embodied was passed in 1792, when judges or justices were authorised to order any prisoner on discharge to be conveyed by pass to his parish, where, of course, he had a claim to be cared for; and in the Gaol Act of 1823 the visiting justices of any prison were authorised to forward prisoners to places where they could find employment, the funds to be provided from bequests and benefactions belonging to the gaol, or from the rates.

In 1802 societies began to be established for the purpose of aiding prisoners on discharge, and in 1862 these societies were recognised by statute in such manner that the justices might hand over to them the money they devoted to the purpose of aiding prisoners, to be appropriated to finding employment for them, and enabling them by loans and grants of money to live by honest labour.

In 1857 a society was established for aiding prisoners discharged from penal servitude, and has successfully carried on those most useful duties since that time.

When the local prisons were transferred to Government in 1878 there existed twenty-nine of these institutions connected with prisons in England and Wales, six in Scotland, and only two in Ireland. As many prisons had no Aid Society in connection with them a great many prisoners left prison without any chance of the aid the justices had been encouraged by these Acts to afford them.

Since the above date, however, a uniform system has been applied in all localities, and the formation of Aid Societies has been so much encouraged that there are now sixty-three Discharged Prisoners' Aid Societies, working in connection with all prisons in England and Wales except one or two, besides forty-two other societies, refuges, and homes. The funds with which these societies work are derived from the gratuities granted to the prisoners under the system of progressive stages, already described, and from an additional grant made by the Government out of a sum of £4000 voted annually. This is distributed among the prisons in proportion to the number of prisoners to be helped, but with a proviso that an equal amount shall be provided by private subscription as a guarantee of that local and private interest in the work without which not only it cannot prosper, but evidently might even have a positively mischievous effect, by creating a presumption that "Government" admitted it to be within its proper functions to find employment on discharge for any person who came into prison.

The sum expended in 1884-85 in gratuities to prisoners amounted to £7280, besides the private subscriptions or proceeds of charities and bequests administered by the Discharged Prisoners' Aid Societies. The expenditure by the local authorities in 1875, 1876, and 1877 amounted on the average of the three years to £1791 per annum, and it is reasonable to claim as one of the improvements since 1878 that of introducing throughout the country the practice which before was for the most part confined to the most enlightened among the local bodies.

## CHAPTER VIII.

### THE PREVENTIVE SYSTEM—JUVENILES—REFORMATORIES —INDUSTRIAL SCHOOLS.

In the downward path which leads to habitual crime the first step is the most important, and to arrest the victim before he takes it the most effectual check on his adoption of that career. In a correspondence between Lord Shaftesbury and Mr. Clay, Chaplain of Preston prison in 1853, are given some statistical observations, framed from the best information Mr. Clay could obtain of the age at which the criminal career of those who came under his observations had commenced. He says they "indicate a statistical law nearly of the same character as you have observed. In looking over my numerous MS. narratives, written or dictated by prisoners, I am led to believe (in respect to actual though undetected delinquency) that 58 per cent first practised dishonesty when under fifteen.

14 per cent between fifteen and sixteen.
8 „ under seventeen, eighteen, or nineteen.
20 „ under twenty."

In short, according to these observations, most criminals commenced dishonesty when under twenty years of age, and more than half when under fifteen. Clearly, then, preventive measures applied below these ages might reasonably be expected to effect a great check on the development of crime.

Those who were concerned in dealing with crime in the early part of this century commonly remarked on the dimensions which juvenile criminality was attaining to. Statistics supported their opinions.

The only preventive measures were the Apprenticeship Laws of the time of Henry VIII., under which children between five and thirteen found begging or idle were compulsorily bound apprentices to some handicraft.

The training in vice was systematic; young people were employed for the double reason that they could operate in many positions in which an adult would find less facility; and further, the penalty of capital punishment would not usually be inflicted on detection. Boys of twelve, fourteen, and sixteen were, however, sometimes hanged; and a child named Leary—who commenced at the age of eight by stealing apples, and progressing through theft of tarts and loaves, robberies of tills, and of trunks, etc. from carts, to burglary, at length becoming the head of a gang—was, at the age of thirteen, sentenced to be hanged, but eventually got off with transportation for life. There were said to be in London 200 flash houses frequented by 6000 boys and girls who had no employment or means of livelihood but by thieving.

In 1816, when the population of London was under a million and a half, there were in London prisons above 3000 inmates under twenty years of age—half of these were under seventeen, some were nine or ten, and 1000 of these children were convicted of felony. These ages correspond very closely with those referred to above as the result of the later observations of Lord Shaftesbury and Mr. Clay.

The full force of these figures will not be felt unless we contrast with them the statistics of the present day, which show that in all England and Wales, with a population of about twenty-seven millions, there were on 31st March 1884 only 275 prisoners under sixteen years of age, and 3226 between sixteen and twenty-one; a considerable number of both these being, no doubt, in prison temporarily in compliance with the law which requires that the prison shall be the channel by which they shall be sent to a reformatory.

It is clear enough that to place young people of such an age in ordinary prisons with adult prisoners—especially under the imperfect system of discipline then existing, and with the great facilities for contamination by association which prisons then afforded—not only was not calculated to check their criminal tendencies, but rather to develop them, and to deprive the prison of the dread which it ought to inspire. In fact, the system which then prevailed of employing prisoners as wardsmen in positions of authority, would seem to have been almost designed for the purpose of exalting the habitual criminal in the eyes of these young tyros on the profession. As the sins of the fathers are in these matters very decidedly visited on the children, it may be said that the present and past generation have been suffering from the neglect of the one which preceded them to take notice in time of these warnings.

It was not likely that these truths had escaped the observation of philanthropists before the times above referred to. The Marine Society for clothing waifs and strays and sending them to sea commences its history in 1756. In the list of reformatory and preventive institutions existing in 1884 the earliest founded appears to be the Philanthropic Society's Farm School at Redhill, which was founded in 1788 or 1789—eleven years after Howard published his *State of Prisons.* Some few other institutions of the same kind were no doubt established soon after, and their promoters were encouraged by official co-operation, so that in the Parkhurst Act, 1838, it is recited that "Her Majesty has lately exercised Her Royal Prerogative of Mercy in granting Pardon to young offenders who have been sentenced to Transportation or Imprisonment upon the condition of placing himself or herself under the care of some Charitable Institution for the reception and reformation of young offenders named in such pardon, and conforming to and abiding by the orders and rules thereof, and whereas the same has been found beneficial, and whereas it is expedient that some provision should be made for carrying the same more fully into effect," etc. The law then enacted made the escape of such offenders from such institutions, or refusal to abide by the rules thereof, punishable by imprisonment and forfeiture of the pardon, and in this way adopted them as in a certain sense Government institutions, armed with the authority which belongs to the executive power.

The first completely official establishment in England of a prison for young offenders in which to apply to juveniles a system of treatment distinguished from that applied to adults, by being composed more largely of the reforming than the strictly penal element, was when Parkhurst prison, as already stated, was established for juvenile offenders sentenced to transportation or imprisonment. The preamble of this Act, passed 10th August 1838, observed that it might "be of great public advantage that a prison be provided in which young offenders may be detained and corrected, and receive such Instructions and be subject to such Discipline as shall appear most conducive to their Reformation and to the Repression of Crime," and that "the buildings of Parkhurst in the Isle of Wight, lately used as a Military Hospital and as a Medical Asylum for the Children of Soldiers," might be "conveniently used for such a Prison."

The Reformatory and Industrial Schools Act subsequently passed supplanted this institution by others established on a system which will be described, so that whereas in 1849 there were about 700 young persons at Parkhurst, in 1854 there were only 536, and on 31st December 1864 only 68—no more than fifteen young convicts having been received in that year, and the number of juveniles sentenced to long terms of imprisonment (who had also since 1854 been received there) did not increase the number enough to justify the retention of the establishment. It was therefore closed in 1864, and since 1866 there have been no juveniles in any Government convict establishment.

The distinction between a reformatory and an industrial school is very important. The first is a place of punishment for a convicted offender, as well as a place of training, and reception into a reformatory must be preceded by a period in prison of not less than ten days. The industrial school, on the other hand, is purely a preventive or training institution, from which the conviction for certain crimes will exclude a child.

Reformatory and industrial schools are not provided by the State, nor is there any obligation on any Local Authority to provide them or contribute to them, or on any Court of Justice to send children to them, or on managers of such schools to receive the children whom the magistrates commit.

A reformatory or industrial school may be established in two ways—(*a*) by private individuals, either as a proprietary institution, or as a charitable institution supported by voluntary contributions; (*b*) in England by a Local Prison Authority as defined by the Prison Act, 1865 (*i.e.* Quarter Sessions in counties and Town Councils in Quarter Session Boroughs), in Scotland by a County Board.

A School Board may also establish an industrial school, and both a Prison Authority and a School Board, or County Board in Scotland, may aid instead of establishing, an industrial school.

Day industrial schools may, in England, be established by the same means as ordinary industrial schools.

The steps by which the present Reformatory System has been established are shown in the abstract of Acts passed from time to time, given in the report of the Royal Commission on the subject, 1884.

## Reformatories up to 1866.

Before 1854 the only children legally detained in a reformatory were those under conditional pardon—the pardon being given on the condition that instead of suffering imprisonment they should be detained in a school of this kind under voluntary management, and not subject to Government rules or under Government inspection. In 1854 was passed the first Reformatory Act applying both to England and Scotland. The reformatory was to be certified by the Secretary of State, and inspected by an Inspector of Prisons. Power was given to the Court convicting the juvenile offender under sixteen to sentence him to detention in a reformatory for not less than two or more than five years, in addition to imprisonment in gaol not less than fourteen days. Treasury contributions for maintenance in whole or in part were authorised, and also compulsory contributions from the parent, not exceeding 5s. per week, which went in relief of treasury charges. In 1855, and again in 1856, the Act was amended in minor details.

In 1857 the Act, so far as England was concerned, was enlarged by enabling, for the first time, Local Authorities—viz. Quarter Sessions in Counties and Councils of Quarter Session Boroughs—to contribute towards the establishment of a reformatory, and the same authorities were likewise empowered to contract for the reception therein of children from the local jurisdiction. By section 13 a valuable modification of the system was introduced, viz.—a power to grant licences to the inmates upon probation after at least half of their period of detention. By section 4 plans of buildings were to be submitted to the Secretary of State.

In the same year the Rev. Sidney Turner was appointed Inspector of Prisons, with special reference to reformatories.

In 1866 the previous Acts were repealed, and the

Consolidating and Amending Act now in force was passed, applying both to England and Scotland, and placing the reformatories of both countries practically on the same footing. The most noticeable changes were that by section 4 a special Inspector of Reformatories was established; by section 12 the Secretary of State was required to make rules for the government of the reformatory; and by section 14 the important limitation of age was introduced, prohibiting an offender under ten from being sent to a reformatory, unless either the sentence was passed at Assizes or Quarter Sessions, or he had been previously charged with an offence punishable with penal servitude or imprisonment.

## INDUSTRIAL SCHOOLS—SCOTLAND.

The first Industrial Schools Act was passed in 1854, and applied to Scotland exclusively. It enabled a Sheriff or Magistrate to commit vagrant children under fourteen, though not charged with any offence, till they were fifteen, to any reformatory or industrial school or other similar institution, whether established by a Parochial Board or an association of individuals. The distinction between a reformatory and industrial school had not then been formulated. The commitment was not to be ordered if the parent gave security for the good behaviour of the child. In the event of the order being made, the parent, if solvent, was bound to pay for the maintenance of the child, and, so far as he was unable to do so, the expense was made recoverable from the Parochial Board of the parish to which the child, if a pauper, would have been chargeable.

The school was to be approved by the Secretary of State; the rules to be confirmed by the Lord Advocate; and the power of granting aid (towards either the erection of the building or the annual expense of the institution) was given to the Education Committee of the Privy Council (s. 7).

In 1855 and 1856 the Act was amended in minor details. In 1861 the Acts of 1854 and 1856 were repealed and replaced by a consolidating statute, in which the principal changes were the following:—

The classes of children admissible were enlarged so as to include not only mendicant and destitute children, but children under twelve, charged with an offence and, refractory children under fourteen; not, however, any who had previously been imprisoned for more than thirty days. Power was given to managers (s. 11) to permit a child to lodge with its parent or any respectable person.

The powers of the Committee of Education were transferred to the Secretary of State, who was to nominate the inspector (s. 4); to approve the rules (s. 17); to recommend the grant to the treasury for maintenance only of inmates (s. 18); and to have power to discharge from the school (s. 15). In certain circumstances (s. 16) the justices also had power to discharge.

The power of the parent to prevent an order being made for the detention of his child by offering security for his good behaviour was not re-enacted. The parent might be ordered to pay up to 5s. per week, and if he applied for committal of a refractory child, had to pay all.

By section 21 the liability of the Parochial Board was limited so as to apply only to a child who was at the time of his detention, or had been within three months from that date, chargeable to the parish, and was to continue only so long as he remained chargeable.

The Act was limited to expire in 1864, but in 1862 it was continued till 1867, and in 1866 the Scotch and English Acts were consolidated.

### INDUSTRIAL SCHOOLS—ENGLAND.

The first Act was passed in 1857, three years later than the Scotch Act.

The school was to be certified by the Committee of Council of Education, and examined by their inspector (s. 3). The children were to be above seven and under fourteen at the date of their committal (s. 2). Detention not to be beyond fifteen. Conviction of vagrancy was to be the initial step (s. 6), and the justices could only make order in default of the parent finding security for the child's good behaviour.

Power was given by sections 12 and 13 to the justices to discharge the child on the application of the parents or managers, if satisfied that employment was provided for him, or that due security was given for his good behaviour. The managers had power by section 17 to allow the child to lodge at the house of his parent or any respectable person.

The parent might, by the order of justices (ss. 15 and 16), be made liable to contribute to the support of the child up to 3s. per week. No liability was imposed on the guardians; but by section 21 they were empowered, with the consent of the Local Government Board, to contract with the managers for the education of any pauper child. No provision was made for any Government contribution. In 1860 the powers of the Council of Education were transferred to the Secretary of State.

In 1861 (the same year in which was passed the Consolidating Act as to Scotch Industrial Schools) these Acts were repealed by a consolidating enactment. The two principal changes were, that power was, by section 17, given to the Treasury to contribute towards the maintenance of the children any sum that the Secretary of State might recommend; and that the contributions of the parents imposed by justices might, by section 18, be as much as 5s. per week, and was required to be for the full expense, where the child was a refractory child sent at the instance of the parents. Rules were to be approved by the Secretary of State (s. 13). The limit of the age of seven was not re-enacted. The condition of conviction and the classes admissible to industrial schools were enlarged, so as to include not only destitute and mendicant children, but children charged with an offence, and refractory children. Those, however, who had previously been convicted of felony were excluded.

The Act was limited to expire in 1864, but in 1862 it was re-enacted, and in 1866 the English and Scotch Acts were consolidated.

## INDUSTRIAL SCHOOLS—ENGLAND AND SCOTLAND.

In 1866 the English and Scotch Acts were consolidated by an Act now in force, the effects of which was to place the industrial schools of both countries on the same footing. An industrial school is one in which industrial training is provided, and in which children are lodged, clothed, and fed, as well as taught. The mode of establishing an industrial school has already been described. The same person is to be appointed by the Secretary of State to be the Inspector of Industrial Schools and the Inspector of Reformatories. Assistant Inspectors may also be appointed.

On the Inspector's report the Secretary of State may, if the managers desire it, certify an industrial school as one to which children may be compulsorily sent under the Act. The managers may resign this certificate, or the Secretary of State may withdraw it; in either case it ceases to have the privileges of an industrial school.

Contributions may be made by the Local Authority —viz., the Prison Authority of Counties and Boroughs in England and the County Board in Scotland—towards the building of an industrial school and towards the maintenance and management of it. Since 1872 they have been empowered to establish and undertake them themselves, and to contribute to the ultimate disposal of the inmates. Plans of schools and of additions and alterations must be first approved by the Secretary of State.

The rules of the school are made by the managers, but must be approved by the Secretary of State; and a child above ten years old not conforming thereto may be imprisoned for from fourteen days to three months, and sent thence to a reformatory school.

If the child escapes it may be sent back to the school

for a longer period of time, and if above ten years of age may further be imprisoned as above and sent to a reformatory school. Assisting a child to escape is also penal, involving £20 penalty and imprisonment with or without hard labour for not more than two months. The Treasury may contribute towards the custody and maintenance of the children, such contributions not to exceed 2s. per head per week in the case of children committed on the application of their own friends. The local authorities also contribute to the maintenance of children sent to the school by them, and the parent or person legally liable to maintain the child must, if the magistrates determine that he is able, contribute a sum not exceeding 5s. per week, such payments to go in relief of the charges on the Treasury.

A defaulter can be distrained on, or, if this is ineffectual, imprisoned.

Section 38 applies only to Scotland, and provides that when a child at the time he is sent to an industrial school, or within three months previous, has been chargeable to any parish, the parochial board and inspector of the poor of the parish of the settlement of the child, if the settlement is in Scotland, shall, so long as he continues so chargeable, be liable to repay to the Treasury all expenses incurred in maintaining him in school to an amount not exceeding 5s. per week.

The class of children who may be committed to an industrial school are those who are under fourteen years of age, and who are found begging or receiving alms (actually or under pretext of selling); who are found wandering without settled abode, proper guardianship, or visible means of subsistence; who are found destitute—

either being orphans or having a surviving parent who is undergoing penal servitude or imprisonment; who are children of a woman twice convicted of crime, 34 and 35 Vict. cap. 112; who frequent the company of thieves; or who come under the provisions of the Education Acts described below. If a child under twelve years of age is charged with a punishable offence, and has not previously been convicted of felony, he may be sent to an industrial school. A refractory child under fourteen years of age may, on the application of its guardian, be committed to an industrial school; and a refractory pauper child, or one either of whose parents has been convicted, may be sent to an industrial school.

The school to which a child is to be sent must be willing to receive it. It is selected by the magistrate, and it must be certified, and, if possible, must be conducted in accordance with the religious persuasion to which the child belongs. If a child is committed to a school not so conducted, it may, on application of its nearest friend, be removed to a school so conducted named by the friend, but, in any case, a minister of the child's religious persuasion may visit it and instruct it in religion.

The order of detention in the school must not extend beyond the time when the child is sixteen years old.

The managers may permit a child to lodge outside the school, and may license it for three months at a time to live with a selected person after eighteen months' detention. They may also apprentice it.

1874
37 & 38 Vict.
c. 47.

In 1874 Prison Authorities received power to borrow to meet capital expenditure.

In 1880 the scope of industrial schools was much enlarged to what is at present an unknown extent by authority being given to commit any child under fourteen who is found to be lodging, living, or residing with common or reputed prostitutes, or in a house resided in or frequented by prostitutes for the purpose of prostitution, or to be frequenting the company of prostitutes. 1880, 43 & 44 Vict. c. 15.

In 1870 was passed the Elementary Education Act, providing for the establishment of School Boards. This has opened a new phase in the history of industrial schools so far as concerns England. To School Boards were given the same powers of contributing to the establishment and maintenance of industrial schools which Prison Authorities possessed under section 12 of the Act of 1866, and also powers which Prison Authorities then did not possess of themselves establishing industrial schools. They did not, however, receive the powers which Prison Authorities had under section 36 of the Act of 1866, to contract for the maintenance of children. 1870, 33 & 34 Vict. c. 75, ss. 27, 28.

By section 36 they were empowered, if they thought fit, to appoint an officer to take steps to have children sent to industrial schools, *i.e.* to enforce the Industrial Schools Act in their district.

In 1872, by the Education (Scotland) Act, School Boards were enabled to establish and maintain certified industrial schools. 35 & 36 Vict. c. 62, s. 41.

The Elementary Education Act, 1876, carried the movement still further in England:— 1876, 39 & 40 Vict. c. 79.

(*a*) By multiplying the number of children sent to Industrial Schools.

(*b*) By the introduction of *day* Industrial Schools.

The multiplication of the number of children sent to Industrial Schools was effected by two enactments:—

(*a*) An enactment (s. 13) making it obligatory on the School Authority (*i.e.* School Boards and School Attendance Committees, section 7) to take steps to send all children to Industrial Schools who were liable to be so sent, unless the School Authority thought it inexpedient. Thus the Industrial Schools Act would be worked to the uttermost.

(*b*) An enactment (ss. 11 and 12) declaring it obligatory on the School Authorities to apply to the justices for orders compelling the attendance at a public elementary school of children over five and under fourteen, whose elementary education was habitually neglected by their parents, or who were found habitually wandering or consorting with criminals or disorderly persons, and enabling the justices on the breach of such a school attendance order to commit the child to an Industrial School (in the event of there being no suitable *day* Industrial School as hereinafter mentioned).

The effect of these enactments was somewhat modified by the provision of section 14, relaxing the restrictions on the licence so as to authorise a licence to be granted in the case of a child sent at the instance of a School Board to an industrial school at any time after the lapse of one month (instead of eighteen months as in other cases), and this whether the child came within the provisions of the Industrial Schools Acts or was sent merely for the breach of an attendance order.

Middlesex has an Industrial School regulated by Local Acts, 17 and 18 Vict. c. clxix., and 38 and 39 Vict. c. lxxxvii.

## Certified Day Industrial Schools.

Day Industrial Schools, *i.e.* schools where the managers provide industrial training, elementary education, and one or more meals a day, but not lodging, were authorised by the Elementary Education Act, 1876, which applies only to England; and by 41 and 42 Vict. cap. xxi. for Glasgow.

At present there are ten such schools established by School Boards in England and two in Glasgow.

The former are regulated (1) by the Act of 1876; (2) by an Order in Council, 20th March 1877, which was made under the powers of that Act and which applied to them with certain modifications, the provisions of the Acts relating to Boarding Industrial Schools; (3) by an Order, 4th January 1878, made by the Secretary of State also under the Act of 1876; (4) by the general regulations which he makes for their governance; (5) by recommendations of the Secretary of State of 9th August 1881 as to Parliamentary grants; and (6) by a Supplementary Order in Council (as to licenses) of 25th October 1881.

The general result is as follows:—

Both Prison Authorities and School Boards have the same powers of establishing or contributing to a day industrial school as they have in the case of boarding industrial schools.

The school may be used for various classes of children :—

I.—Children under detention—

(*a*) Any child who, under the Industrial Schools Act, might be sent to a boarding industrial school may be sent to a day industrial school unless he is a child without a home or destitute, or a refractory child sent from the workhouse, cases to which a day school is manifestly inappropriate.

(*b*) A child between five and fourteen may, for breach of an order requiring him to attend school under the Elementary Education Act, 1876, be sent to a day industrial school, but such an attendance order can only be made on a child who is either—

(1) Under the Act prohibited from being taken into full-time employment, and the parent must habitually and without reasonable excuse have neglected to provide sufficient elementary instruction for it; or

(2) A child found habitually wandering, or not under proper control, or in the company of rogues, vagabonds, disorderly persons, or reputed criminals.

*These children are sent by order of the Court, which authorises their detention during certain hours of the day. Order to be for not more than three years nor after the age of fourteen.*

II.—Children not under detention—

(*a*) A child may attend the day industrial school by agreement between the managers, the School Authority, and the parent, in pursuance of an attendance order made by justices on the complaint of the School Authority.

(*b*) A child may attend not in pursuance of any order of the Court, but by agreement with the managers at the joint request of the Local Authority and the parent.

*These children are not liable to compulsory detention. Order to be for not more than one year or beyond the age of fourteen.*

The expense of maintenance in day industrial schools is taken to be 3s. or 3s. 6d. per week. This expense is met partly by the Treasury contributions, partly by the contributions from the parent or guardians, and the residue is made up by the managers.

For children under detention the Treasury contribution has been fixed by the Secretary of State practically at about 1s. per week, being the maximum allowed by the statute. Contribution has to be made by the parent according to his ability, not exceeding 2s. per week. This sum is collected by the School Board, and paid over to the managers and not to the Treasury. If the parent is unable to pay, the guardians are bound to give him relief sufficient to enable him to pay what, in their opinion, he cannot pay for himself.

For children not under detention the Treasury contribution has been fixed by the Secretary of State practically at 6d. per week, being the maximum allowed by the statute. The parent's contribution, which goes to the managers, is fixed by agreement between him and the managers, but it must be between 1s., the minimum named by the Act, and 2s., the maximum authorised by the Secretary of State. Nothing in any case is paid by the guardians.

The statute, however, sanctions Treasury contributions only subject to conditions made by the Secretary of State, and requires that one of these conditions should provide for examination of the children in the standards of proficiency applicable to the Parliamentary grant in public elementary schools. The conditions now in force were issued on 9th August 1881.

After one month's detention managers may, with consent of the Local Authority, grant a license on condition of the child attending a public elementary school, or (in default) a certified efficient school. License to be for not more than three months, but to be renewable; to be revocable by the managers. (Order in Council, 25th October 1881.)

The provisions as to inspecting, certifying, building, altering the buildings, and making rules for reformatory schools, are substantially the same as for industrial schools; the expenses also are met in the same way, partly from private funds, partly from local rates, and partly from funds provided by the Treasury, and partly by contributions enforced from the parents or guardians.

The class of offenders who may be sent to a reformatory are those who, being under sixteen years old, are convicted and sentenced to ten days' imprisonment or more, but a child of under ten may be sent only if he has previously been charged with a crime or offence, or is sentenced by a judge or Court of General Quarter Sessions.

The school is selected by the Court which sentences, or by a visiting justice of the prison he is committed to, and the provisions to secure religious teaching according to the offender's persuasion, are the same as in the case of industrial schools.

The provisions as to licensing an offender committed to a reformatory school, and the penalties for escaping, either from the school or while on license, are similar to those which apply to industrial schools, the period of imprisonment for such offenders not to exceed three months, and persons assisting in an offender's escape are liable to £20 penalty and imprisonment, with or without hard labour, for a term not exceeding two months.

A young offender sentenced to penal servitude and imprisonment may have the sentence commuted to detention in a reformatory for any period from two years to five years.

In 1874 prison authorities were enabled to borrow to meet capital expenses of reformatory schools.

The Prison Act, 1877, which transferred local prisons to the State, expressly saved the power of prison authorities to contribute to reformatories.

In the case of reformatories the nominal treasury contribution, made on the recommendation of the Secretary of State, is 6s. per week for each child, out of a total average cost of about 8s. This contribution, however, is reduced to 4s. for any child who has completed three years' detention, and has attained sixteen.

The committing authority (*i.e.* the county magistrates or the town council) makes, as a rule by agreement with the managers, a grant of 1s. 6d. or 2s. 6d. a week for each case sent by them.

The parent can be ordered by the justices to contribute up to 5s. per week, though the actual contribution, in the great majority of cases where any payment is made, is about 1s. All such payments go in relief of the Treasury. The residue of the expense of maintenance falls on the managers. It has been determined by the Law Courts that the expense of removing the child from the gaol to the reformatory, and of providing him with a proper suit of clothes, has been transferred by the Prison Act, 1877, from the Local Authorities to the Treasury. The Treasury accordingly makes a clothing allowance of £1 on admission; also an allowance for cases on license of 2s. a week for thirteen weeks, and 1s. a week for the next twenty-six weeks.

The statistics of the expense of these schools between the years 1859-1882 are as follows :—

| Year. | No. in School exclusive of those on License. | Paid by Treasury. | Parents. | Rates. | Subscriptions and Legacies. | Total School Expenditure. |
|---|---|---|---|---|---|---|
| | | £ | £ | £ | £ | £ |
| 1859 | 3276 | 57,681 | 1604 | 2,602 | 16,169 | 72,893 |
| 1869 | 5480 | 82,357 | 3240 | 18,042 | 7,730 | 118,419 |
| 1882 | 6601 | 87,242 | 5918 | 23,711 | 5,956 | 134,204 |

Mr. Rogers estimates the total ordinary cost of reformatories per head at 7s. 6d. to 8s. per week, or £19 : 10s. or £20 : 16s. per annum, and the parents' average share of the burden at £1 per annum, or 5 per cent.

| | | | |
|---|---|---|---|
| The Treasury, at 6s. per week, gives . . | £15 | 12 | 0 |
| Less parents' contribution . . . . . | 1 | 0 | 0 |
| | 14 | 12 | 0 |
| Add average clothing allowance . . . | 0 | 8 | 0 |
| Total ordinary contribution from the State . | £15 | 0 | 0 |

In the case of industrial schools the Treasury contribution is made on the recommendation of the Secretary of State, and has been varied from time to time.

The present scale is as follows, out of a total cost of about 7s., or in the case of schoolships 8s. :—

For any child above ten years of age, 5s. or 3s. 6d., according as the school was established before or after 1st March 1872, and this allowance in either case is reduced to 3s. for any child who fulfils the double conditions of being fifteen years of age, and of having been four years in detention.

For any child in ships (except the London School Board ship *Shaftesbury*, established after March 1872), 6s.

The exceptional rates are :—

| | *s.* | *d.* | |
|---|---|---|---|
| For any child sent under sub-section 2 of section 11 of the Elementary Education Act, 1876 . . . . . . . . . | 3 | 6 | per week. |
| For any child between six and ten years of age . . . . . . . . . | 3 | 0 | ,, |

| | *s.* | *d.* | |
|---|---|---|---|
| For any child employed outside the school during the whole day, provided he earns at least 2s. 6d. a week . . . . . | 2 | 6 | per week. |
| For any child sent for breach of an attendance order under sub-section 1 of section 11 of the Elementary Education Act . | 2 | 0 | ,, |
| For any refractory child sent by its parents | 2 | 0 | ,, |
| For any refractory child sent by a workhouse or pauper school . . . . | 0 | 0 | ,, |
| For any child under six years of age . . | 0 | 0 | ,, |

An allowance is also made to certificated teachers after a year's approved service, viz. :—

| | Male. | Female. |
|---|---|---|
| For a teacher holding a parchment certificate . . . . . . | £20 | £15. |
| For a teacher not holding a parchment certificate . . . . . . | £15 | £10. |

The parent can be ordered by the justices to contribute up to 5s. per week, but any payment which he makes goes in relief of the Treasury. The committing authority makes weekly grants for each case sent under agreement with the managers. These vary from 2s. 6d. to 1s. 6d. from the Magistrates, and from 1s. 6d. to 7s. from the School Boards.

In England no charge can be imposed on the poor rate except where School Boards draw their precepts from it—or children are committed at the instance of school attendance committees; or refractory pauper children are sent on the application of the guardians. In Scotland, when a child, at the time of his being sent to school, or within three months then last past, has been chargeable to any parish or Parochial Board, the inspector of the poor of the parish of the settlement of such child (if the settlement of the child is in any parish in Scotland) is, so long as he continues to be chargeable, liable to repay to the Treasury all expenses incurred in maintaining him, not exceeding 5s. per week.

The residue of any expense not defrayed from any of these sources falls on the managers. There is no clothing allowance from the Treasury, nor any allowance for cases on license.

The statistics of expenditure in the industrial schools for the years 1864-1882 are as follows :—

| Year. | No. in School exclusive of those on License. | Paid by Treasury. | Parents and Parochial Boards. | Rates. | School Board. | Subscriptions. | Total Expenditure. |
|---|---|---|---|---|---|---|---|
| | | £ | £ | £ | £ | £ | £ |
| 1864 | 1,668 | 15,887 | 1,189 | .. | .. | .. | .. |
| 1869 | 6,974 | 74,102 | 3,607 | 21,057 | .. | 33,741 | 138,408 |
| 1874 | 11,409 | 134,333 | 9,093 | 20,651 | 19,925 | 48,608 | 252,845 |
| 1882 | 17,461 | 170,473 | 16,993 | 42,727 | 59,584 | 30,919 | 338,200 |

Mr. Rogers estimates the total ordinary cost of industrial schools per head at 7s. to 7s. 6d. per week, or £18 : 5s. to £19 : 10s. per annum, and the parents' average share of the burden (including the Parochial Board payments in Scotland) at a little more than £1 per annum, or 5 per cent.

| | | | |
|---|---|---|---|
| In 5s. cases the Treasury gives . . . . | £13 | 0 | 0 |
| Less parents' and Parochial Board's payments . | 1 | 0 | 0 |
| Net cost to Treasury . . . | £12 | 0 | 0 |

| | | | |
|---|---|---|---|
| But the average cost to the Treasury is about . | £11 | 5 | 0 |
| Less parents' and Parochial Board's payments . | 1 | 0 | 0 |
| Net cost to Treasury . . . | £10 | 5 | 0 |

The action of the Reformatory Schools in respect to the number of juveniles taken in hand by them, and their cost, is shown by the following figures from the Report of the Royal Commission, 1884:—

| | | |
|---|---|---|
| Admitted from 1854 to 1881 inclusive | 32,575 *males*, | 7754 *females* |
| Discharged— | | |
| To employment or service . . | 8,857 ,, | 3422 ,, |
| To friends . . . . . . | 8,679 ,, | 1959 ,, |
| Emigrated . . . . . . | 2,108 ,, | 133 ,, |
| Sent to sea . . . . . . | 3,924 ,, | ... ,, |
| Enlisted . . . . . . | 631 ,, | ... ,, |
| As diseased . . . . . . | 347 ,, | 166 ,, |
| As incorrigible . . . . | 202 ,, | 89 ,, |
| Transferred . . . . . . | 680 ,, | 274 ,, |
| Died . . . . . . . | 729 ,, | 280 ,, |
| Absconded . . . . . . | 898 ,, | 220 ,, |

While there remained on 31st December 1880—

| | | |
|---|---|---|
| In school . . . . . . | 4571 *males*, | 1067 *females* |
| On license . . . . . . | 870 ,, | 137 ,, |
| In prison . . . . . . | 16 ,, | 1 ,, |
| Absconded . . . . . . | 63 ,, | 16 ,, |

The Report from which these figures are derived also states that the number of children in ordinary Industrial Schools on 30th September 1881 was 15,798.

The Statutes in force in Ireland differ from those which apply to Great Britain in some respects.

## Difference between the Reformatory Acts in Ireland and Great Britain.

| English Act, 29 & 30 Vict. c. 117. | Irish Act, 31 & 32 Vict. c. 59. | |
|---|---|---|
| Sect. 14 . | Sect. 12 . | I. The minimum sentence of imprisonment to be passed on a young offender, previously to being sent to a reformatory in England, is ten days. In Ireland it is fourteen. |
| Sect. 18 . | Sect. 26 . | II. Managers of reformatory schools in England may grant licenses for three months to young offenders after the expiration of eighteen months of the reformatory sentence. In Ireland not until they have completed half the period of sentence, and then the license may be for twelve months. (In Great Britain the Treasury makes an allowance to managers of reformatories of 2s. a week for thirteen weeks, and 1s. per week for twenty-six weeks for each inmate of their school that is placed out on license. This allowance is not granted to managers of reformatories in Ireland.) |
| Sects. 20 and 21 . | Sect. 19 . | III. In England young offenders who have been sentenced to imprisonment for absconding or wilful breach of rules in the reformatory are liable to be detained in the school for a period equal to so much of the sentence as remained unexpired at the time of his escape or misconduct. In Ireland, when the period of the original reformatory school sentence has expired, the young offender must be discharged from the school irrespective of the time he has been absent as an absconder or in prison. |
| Sect. 14 . Clause 4 Clause 5 | Sect. 12 . ... | IV. In Ireland the clauses which require a young offender to be sent to a school under the exclusive management of persons of the same religious persuasion as the parents of the child, are much more strict than in England, and the inmates of the school must all be of the same religious persuasion as the managers. In England the statute does not contemplate the same strictness, and children of different religions may be inmates of the same school. The 14th section of the English Act, however, directs that a minister of the same religion as the juvenile may visit and instruct him each day at a certain |

| English Act, 29 & 30 Vict. c. 117. | Irish Act, 31 & 32 Vict. c. 59. | |
|---|---|---|
| Clause 5 | | hour to be fixed by the Secretary of State. This clause does not exist in the Irish Act. |
| Sect. 4 . | ... | VI. No substantial addition or alteration shall be made to or in the buildings of a certified reformatory in England without the approval in writing of the Secretary of State. No similar clause exists in the Irish Statute. |
| Sect. 14 . Clause 2 | ... | IX. An offender under ten years of age can only be sent to a reformatory school in England by a judge of assizes or a court of quarter sessions, or in Scotland by a circuit justiciary or sheriff, unless the juvenile had been previously charged with an offence punishable with penal servitude or imprisonment. No such clause exists in the Irish Act. |
| Sect. 12 . | ... | X. In England the managers of a reformatory may make rules to be submitted to the Secretary of State for his approval in writing before being enforced. This clause is omitted in the Irish Act. When appointed inspector of reformatory schools I drew up rules for the management of reformatories, which, however, not having legal power to enforce, were not accepted by the managers. |
| Sects. 20 and 21 . | Sect. 19 . | XI. Young offenders who abscond or are refractory can be imprisoned for six months in Ireland, but only for three months in England. |
| Sect. 25 . | Sect. 24 . | XIV. In England the Secretary of State can remit payment of parental moneys. In Ireland the presiding justices only have that power. |
| Sect. 32 . | ... | XVI. In England the Secretary of State may send a young offender sentenced to penal servitude or imprisonment, on conditional pardon, to a reformatory for a period of not less than two or more than five years. This clause is not in the Irish Act. |
| Sect. 28 . | ... | XXVIII. A prison authority in England may contribute towards the cost of the purchase of land for the site of a reformatory school, the establishment or building of the school, the alteration, enlargement, or rebuilding of a certified reformatory. No such powers are given in the Irish Act. |
| 35 & 36 Vict. c. 21. Sect. 4 . | ... ... | A prison authority in England may themselves undertake any work towards which they are authorised by Act 29 & 30 Vict. c. 117 to contribute, viz., the alteration, enlargement, or rebuilding of a certified reformatory school, or towards the support |

| English Act, 29 & 30 Vict. c. 118. | Irish Act, 31 & 32 Vict. c. 59. | |
|---|---|---|
| 35 & 36 Vict. c. 21. Sect. 4 . | | of the inmates, or towards the management of such school, or towards the establishment or building of a school intended to be a certified reformatory, or towards the purchase of land required either for the use of an existing certified reformatory, or for the site of any school intended to be certified, subject to the provisoes contained in said Act. |
| Sect. 5 . | ... | A prison authority in England may contribute towards the ultimate disposal of any inmate of a certified reformatory established under the Act 35 & 36 Vict. c. 21. The expenses incurred in carrying out this section may be defrayed out of the rates. This Act does not extend to Ireland. |

## Difference between the Irish Industrial Schools Act and the Statutes in Force in Great Britain.

| English Act, 29 & 30 Vict. c. 118. | Irish Act, 31 Vict. c. 25. | |
|---|---|---|
| Sect. 11 . <br> Sect. 13 . | ... <br> ... | II. In Great Britain no substantial addition or alteration can be made to or in the buildings of a certified industrial school without the approval in writing of the Secretary of State. Plans and estimates to be sent to him for his approval. No such clause exists in the Irish Act, nor is it necessary, as the building must, in Ireland, be erected by managers at their own expense, there being no legal authority to defray the cost of buildings out of local rates as in other parts of the United Kingdom; besides, in Ireland the numbers in the schools are limited by the rules, and not by the amount of accommodation provided. |
| Sect. 12 . | ... | III. In Great Britain a prison authority may contribute towards the alteration, enlargement, or rebuilding of a certified school, or towards the establishment of a school intending to be certified, or for the purchase of land, either for the use of an existing school or a school intended to be certified, or to- |

| ENGLISH ACT, 29 & 30 Vict. c. 118. | IRISH ACT, 31 Vict. c. 25. | |
|---|---|---|
| Sect. 12 . | | wards the management of a school, or the support of the inmates. |
| Act 35 & 36 Vict. c. 21. Sects. 7, 8, and 9. | ... | Under the Act 35 & 36 Vict. c. 21, in England the prison authority may themselves purchase land for the site or use of an industrial school. They may establish, build, alter, or enlarge the school, and may pay for its management and the support of the inmates out of public rates. They may contribute to the ultimate disposal of the inmates; and if in a borough, the school may, under certain circumstances, be transferred to a School Board. |
| | | In Scotland a County Board may contribute to any certified industrial school, with the consent, and in the manner provided by the Prisons (Scotland) Administration Act, 1860, respecting contributions to reformatories. |
| | Sect. 9 . | In Ireland the grand jury of a county, or of the county of a town, or the town councils of the boroughs of Dublin, Cork, and Limerick, may appoint a committee to enter into an agreement with the managers of a certified industrial school for the reception, maintenance, and keeping in such school of children ordered to be sent from such county or borough in consideration of such periodical payments as may be agreed upon with such managers. The 10th section directs how the money is to be raised. These are the only sections in the Industrial Schools Act (Ireland), which authorise money to be contributed out of local rates towards the support or maintenance of children in industrial schools. |
| Sect. 36 . | ... | In England a prison authority may also contract with managers for the reception and maintenance of children sent from the district of the prison authority. |
| Sect. 37 . | ... | IV. In Great Britain the guardians of the poor of a union, or the board of managers of a district pauper school, or the parochial board of a parish, may, with the consent of the Poor Law Board in England and Board of Supervision in Scotland, contribute such sums as they think fit towards the maintenance of the children in certified industrial schools admitted on their application. No similar provision is contained in the Irish Act. |
| Sect. 38 . | ... | V. In Scotland the parochial board and inspector of the poor of the parish of the settlement of a child |

| English Act, 29 & 30 Vict. c. 118. | Irish Act, 31 Vict. c. 25. | |
|---|---|---|
| Sect. 38 . | | are liable to repay the Treasury all expenses incurred in maintaining a child in an industrial school, not exceeding 5s. per week, which can be recovered in a summary manner before a magistrate. No such clause exists in the Irish Act. |
| Sect. 16 . | ... | VI. If a parent or step-parent or guardian of a child under fourteen years of age represents to two justices in England, or to a magistrate in Scotland, that he is unable to control the child, the magistrates may |
| Sect. 35 . | ... | send the child to an industrial school. The contribution by the Treasury cannot exceed 2s. per week for such child. These clauses are not in the Irish Act. |
| Sect. 17 . | ... | VII. On it being represented to two justices, or a magistrate, by poor law guardians or the managers of a district pauper school, or by a parochial board, that a pauper child, under fourteen years of age, is refractory, or is the child of parents either of whom has been convicted of a crime, or offence punishable with penal servitude or imprisonment, and that it is desirable that he be sent to an industrial school, the Bench may order him to be sent to such a school. No such clause exists in the Irish Act. |
| Sect. 18 . | ... | VIII. In England, when determining the school to which a child is to be sent, the magistrates are required to endeavour to ascertain the religious persuasion to which the child belongs, and if possible select a school conducted in accordance with such |
| Sect. 20 . | ... | religious persuasion of the child. Should the school be not conducted in accordance with the religious persuasion to which the child belongs, a power of appeal is granted to the parent, step-parent, or nearest relative of the child, against the decision of the Bench, and upon proof of such child's religious persuasion, the application of the appellant, who may name another certified school in Great Britain to which he desires the child to be sent, shall be granted if made within thirty days. |
| | Sects. 14 and 15. | In Ireland no child can legally be sent to any industrial school except one under the exclusive management of persons of the same religious persuasion as the parents or guardians of the child, or that to which the child belongs. Under the 15th section a power of appeal is granted similar to that in the English Act. |

| English Act, 29 & 30 Vict. c. 118. | Irish Act, 31 Vict. c. 25. | |
|---|---|---|
| Sect. 40 . | ... | IX. In Scotland orders for parental contribution for the maintenance of their children in an industrial school shall have the effect of an order made in each week for payment of the amount, and magistrates are authorised to grant order of arrestment under which it is lawful to arrest weekly for payment of such weekly sum, the arrestment to attach not only to the wages due and payable, but also to the wages current. In Ireland no person can be arrested for a debt incurred under the Industrial Schools Act for the support of his child. |
| Sect. 50 . | ... | XII. Expenses incurred in England by a prison authority, or in Scotland by a county board, are defrayed under the provisions of the Prisons Act, 1865, and the Prisons (Scotland) Administration Act. No similar provision is in the Irish Act. |

In Ireland the cost to the public of reformatories was thus apportioned in the year 1881, the number of inmates being about 1149 :—

| Treasury. | Rates. | Subscriptions. | Profits. |
|---|---|---|---|
| £18,125 | £7822 | £529 | £2095 |

Which gives roughly the proportionate cost per inmate: for boys per week 8s. 6d., for girls 10s., thus apportioned on the year's expense :—

| The Treasury. | Rates. | Private Sources. | Profits. |
|---|---|---|---|
| £16 | £7 nearly | 10s. | £2 nearly |

The parents' contribution in 1881 amounted to £663, or say 10s. per head.

The industrial schools, Ireland, cost in 1881 as follows, for about 5750 inmates :—

| Treasury. | Rates. | Subscriptions. | Profits. |
|---|---|---|---|
| £73,437 | £25,073 | £6098 | £9857 |

The parents' contribution in 1881 amounted to £529, or say 2s. per head. These figures may thus be divided and show roughly the proportionate cost per inmate :—

| Treasury. | Rates. | Subscriptions. |
|---|---|---|
| £13 | £4 : 10s. | £1 |

It appears clear, therefore, that in Ireland far more children are sent to industrial schools than in Great Britain in proportion to the population, and that their cost is a heavier burden on the public than in the latter case. The Royal Commission for 1884 say, "It is certain that the certified industrial schools in Ireland are regarded as institutions for poor and deserted children rather than for those of a semi-criminal class, and the result of this feeling is that the managers of many of these institutions refuse to take children who have been found to have committed a criminal offence, and who might legally be convicted of that offence and sent to a reformatory. All taint of criminality having been removed from the schools, numbers of children are sent to them who do not always come under the provision of the Act, and who are sent merely on the ground of destitution. There can be no doubt that many children are sent to the industrial schools in Ireland who would not be so sent in England; whilst in consequence of it, it is to be apprehended that numbers of children who are proper subjects for these institutions are left on the streets as waifs and strays."

# INDEX.

THE END.

*Printed by* R. & R. CLARK, *Edinburgh.*